Passing and Possession Drills

of the
World's Top Teams and Coaches

Edited by
Mike Saif

Published by
WORLD CLASS COACHING

First published April, 2002 by
WORLD CLASS COACHING 9205 W. 131 Terr, Overland Park, KS 66213 (913) 402-0030

ISBN 0-9718218-2-8

Edited by Mike Saif

WORLD CLASS COACHING would like to thank worldofsoccer.com for the use of the graphics

Published by
WORLD CLASS COACHING

Table of Contents

Passing and Possession Drills

of the
World's Top Teams and Coaches

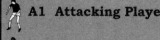 A1 Attacking Player   Path of Player   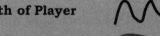 Path of Dribble

 D1 Defending Player   Path of Ball   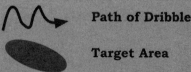 Target Area

Kansas City Wizards

A possession practice contributed by Ken Fogarty, assistant coach, Kansas City Wizards.

Warm-Up
Players are in groups of three, passing and moving over a half-field. Practice different techniques for two to three minutes then stretch after each one.

Techniques
- Give-and-go's
- Takeovers
- Turns

Finish the warm-up with five minutes of ball juggling.

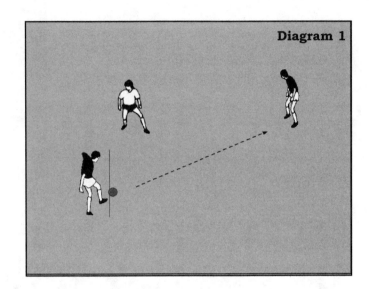

Keep-Away
In the same group of three's, play 2 v 1 in a small area (five yards). Change the defender after one minute.

Coaching Points
- Movement to receive the pass
- Timing of the pass
- Communication
- Defending - pressure and direct the passes

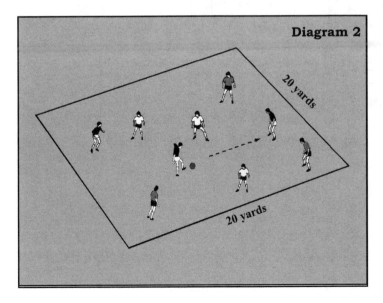

3 v 3 v 3
In a 20 x 20-yard grid, organize into three groups of three players, each group wearing a different colored vest (blue, red and yellow). One group starts off as defenders, the other two groups combine making it 6 v 3 and play keep-away from the defending group. The group that is responsible for losing possession immediately becomes the defenders and play against the other six players.

Coaching Points
- Try to split the defenders
- One touch passes if possible
- Set the pass up for your teammate
- Disguise your passes
- Look beyond the ball

Kansas City Wizards

9 v 9

Play 5 v 5 inside a 40 x 30-yard grid. Four players from each team are positioned around the perimeter. The players inside the grid can use their teammates on the perimeter if they need to. Perimeter players are limited to one touch.

Variation

When the inside player passes to a perimeter player, he follows his pass and changes places with the perimeter player who now becomes part of the 5 v 5 inside the grid.

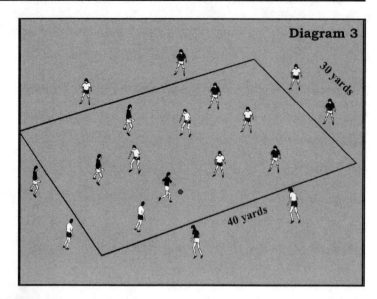

Diagram 3

30 yards

40 yards

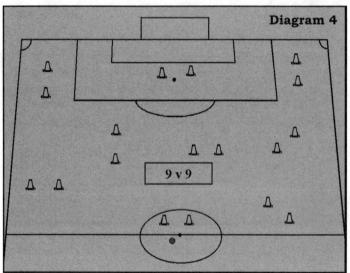

Diagram 4

9 v 9

Half-Field 9 v 9

Place nine sets of small goals using cones or flags on a half-field. Play 9 v 9. Goals can be scored three different ways.

- Ten consecutive passes
- A player dribbling through a goal
- A player passing through a goal to a teammate

Manchester United U19's

In February 1999, I was fortunate enough to spend a day with David Williams, youth team coach at Manchester United. As usual, it was a pleasure to observe Williams work with his players. On this day, the players trained in the morning and afternoon. The morning was a passing and possession session. The afternoon session was spent working on shooting and finishing. When the players practice twice a day, the morning session usually consists of some form of a small-sided game and the afternoon session is usually spent working on technique.

Warm-Up
After a 10-minute jog and stretch, the players quickly got organized into pairs and started passing and moving over a half-field. The players were about 15 yards apart from each other.

Progressions
• The player with the ball dribbles, the player without the ball moves one direction then checks back to receive the pass
• The player without the ball moves away from his partner then quickly turns and checks back to receive the pass
• Add imagination and variation to the passes
• Move to 30 yards apart
• Increase the speed of play

Coaching Point
The receiver has the option of where and when he will move and check back for the ball. Therefore, the player in possession should look up and read the movements of his partner.

Possession
On a marked-out field 60 x 40 yards, play 5 v 5 + 1 with goalkeepers. Each team can score at either end. The goals are not used. A goal can only be scored by a lofted pass from the opposite half of the field and into the goalkeeper's hands without touching the ground. After a goal, the goalkeeper distributes the ball to the scoring team. For example, in diagram 5, the player in possession has just scored by passing a high ball to the goalkeeper's hands. The goalkeeper would then keep the game going by passing the ball back to a player on the dark team. The team in possession can use the goalkeepers to pass back to in order to keep possession. The first 15 minutes were played with a three-touch restriction. The last 10 minutes were played two-touch.

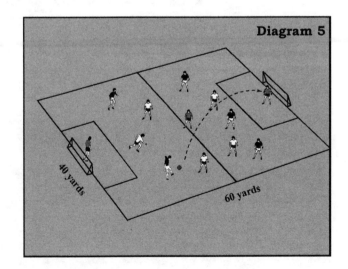

Diagram 5

Coaching Points
• Defensively - mark players
• Defensively - close and pressure to stop the long scoring pass
• Offensively - use the warm-up movements to lose your marker
• Goalkeepers - use feet to control the ball if it hits the ground before it reaches you

Observations
• I saw David Williams do a similar variation of this small-sided game last year. David told me he has many variations of the game that can be used to get across many different coaching points.
• It is a great game to involve the goalkeepers - they get to practice high balls, back-passes, and distribution with both hands and feet.
• The game was played at a quick pace with many one-touch passes.
• Many of the goals that were scored with a one-touch pass were set up by a teammate 'stunning' the ball.
• The players were always aware of their defensive responsibilities.

Manchester United U19's

Half-Field Game

Mark a field with lines extending from the edge of the penalty area to the half-line as shown in diagram 6. Use full size goals and goalkeepers. Play 5 v 5 + 1. A goal can only be scored with a one-touch shot. If the ball goes out-of-bounds, play is restarted with goal-kicks, throw-ins or corner-kicks. Start by playing three-touch. The coach was constantly asking his players to track the other teams' players when they made forward runs.

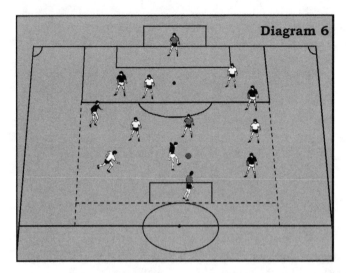

Diagram 6

Progressions

- No restrictions - players are now encouraged to run with the ball if they have a chance. Still one-touch finish to score.
- Each team is shaped in a 2-2-1 formation. Maximum two touches. One touch is used if possible. If two touches are used, the second touch must be a forward touch.
- Add a player and play 6 v 6, no restrictions.

The Liverpool Academy

I observed these sessions of the U11 and U12 youth teams during my visit to the Liverpool Academy early in 1999. The weather was just above freezing but just about all the kids wore shorts and constantly kept on the move to stay warm. The practice was held on the artificial surface at the newly built Liverpool Academy.

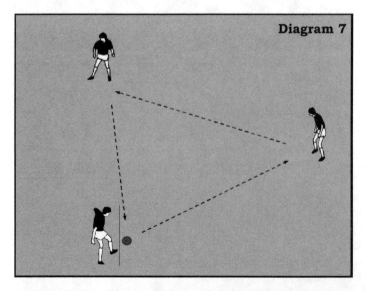

Diagram 7

Warm-Up

The players were organized in threes with one ball per group. Each group formed a 10-yard triangle. The ball was passed in one direction using two touches. The coach was constantly asking the players to take pride in the quality of their passes. He asked them not just to pass in the direction of the player but to pass to a particular foot. The coach also emphasized moving the body into the correct position to receive the pass. After a few minutes, the direction of the passes was changed.

The warm-up was completed with 10 minutes of unopposed 'Coerver' type moves.

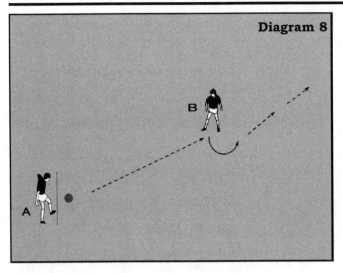

Diagram 8

Pass and Receive

The players are now in pairs. Each pair has a ball and the players are 10 yards apart from each other. This is a simple but effective drill for working on passing and receiving with an open body position.

Player A passes to player B.

Player B controls the ball with an open body position and takes two quick touches away from player A.

Player A follows player B to maintain a 10-yard distance. After his two touches, player B turns and passes to player A who does the same and controls with an open body position.

Progression

Player B moves away then checks back to player A to receive the ball. As player B checks back to receive, he also calls for the pass from player A. This encourages the players to look up and communicate with each other which helps with the timing of their passes.

Progression

The receiving player was then encouraged to 'fake' before he received the ball.

Progression

The players then (still in pairs) worked in a 40 x 40-yard area. The players moved around inside the area passing the ball back-and-forth to their partners.

Coaching Point

Communication was stressed. The passer would tell the receiver whether to hold, turn or pass back depending on the situation.

The players then did two minutes of 1 v 1 keep-away. In this exercise the player in possession attempted to shield the ball from his partner who tried to move around the player with the ball to make him turn and expose the ball.

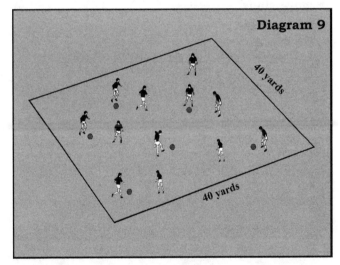

Diagram 9

40 yards

40 yards

Progression

The players then returned to the 40 x 40-yard grid. This time they didn't work in pairs. There were 12 players and six balls. Everyone moved around inside the grid. The players in possession would pass to a player without a ball who would pass it back one-touch at an angle and then peel away and look for another pass from another player.

Coaching Points

• The players were constantly encouraged to be aware of the quality and weight of their passes
• The quality of their first touch and one-touch passes were also stressed

Practice ended with a 30-minute game on a 60 x 40-yard field with small goals and no goalkeepers. The game was stopped only twice for the coach to get across a coaching point. Instead he was encouraging the players throughout the game to focus on the things they had done earlier - passing and receiving.

Venice - Serie 'A'

Observed by Tim Hague who holds an F.A. UEFA 'B' license. Tim has experience teaching and coaching youth soccer in the U.K. and now for three years in northern Italy. This practice was prior to an important 'six pointer' on the road at Lecce. A poor run of only six goals in 10 games had left Venice next to bottom in Serie 'A'. This training session was conducted by the recently appointed coach, Guisepe Materazzi and contained practices for creating space, switching play and creating and finishing goal chances.

One significant observation from my Italian experience is the amount of time allowed for individual ball skills and self tuition/development. The importance of regular practice is emphasized from an early age and the Italian mentality lends itself to the theory of practice makes perfect. It is common to see players of all ages and ability spend some 15 minutes at the start of a practice with a ball each, sometimes unsupervised, just practicing on their own. They will experiment with wall passes using both feet, fakes and moves, juggling and generally getting a better feel for the ball. Technically, the Italians are very good and rarely do you see a player that is uncomfortable on the ball, whatever position they play. Is this partly due to the time spent on individual development? Food for thought!

Warm-Up
Following the individual work, the goalkeepers worked with the goalkeeper coach and the 15 field players split into three teams of five and worked in a 20 x 20-yard area. One team is positioned around the perimeter with a ball each and the other two teams are in pairs inside the grid. The five dark players move around inside the grid playing one touch headers back to a perimeter player and then moving to another server. The white team are active defenders and can challenge their partner for the ball. The teams work for 90 seconds then stretch for two minutes. The players then change roles so that each team takes turns at serving, defending and receiving.

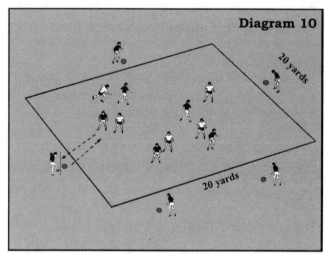

Diagram 10

Progressions
- Jumping to head
- Volleys
- Passes on the ground - using all surfaces of both feet

Coaching Points
- One of the key objectives is to lose your defender
- Keep your head up - be aware
- Good communication
- Quick body movement
- Change direction to create space
- Keep your body between defender and ball
- Quality of service and return passes

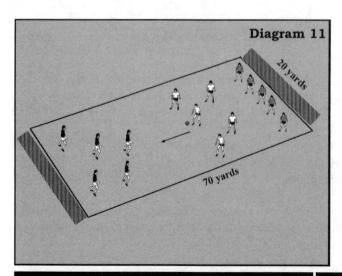

Diagram 11

Three Team Game
Three teams of five players play on a 70 x 20-yard field with 5 -yard end zones at each end. The white team starts with the ball and advances to attack the dark team. The objective is to have control of the ball in the end zone defended by the dark team. If the white team is successful or if they lose possession, the dark team immediately attacks the opposite end zone defended by the gray team and the white team drops back to the end zone vacated by the dark team and gets ready for when play is attacking their end zone later. This proved to be a very demanding game with possession changing hands frequently. Therefore, if a team loses possession in the middle of the field, they must sprint to the end zone they were attacking to get ready to defend again.

Venice - Serie 'A'

The game was played with a two-touch maximum and players were asked to react quickly to a change of possession. The game was played for 20 minutes followed by three minutes of stretching.

Progressions

To encourage more movement off the ball and creating space in a narrow but long area, the coach asked the attacking team to attempt a short pass followed by a long pass whenever possible.
Play one touch

Coaching Points

Good support play
Have a positive attitude to play forward and get into the attacking zone
Be alert to switch from attack to defense - don't switch off
Make it competitive - keep score

10 v 5 Keep-Away

The playing area was lengthened to 85 yards. Two teams of five played keep-away from the other team of five. For example, the white and gray team combine to play against the dark team (defenders). If the defending team wins possession, the team that was responsible for losing possession now become the defenders.

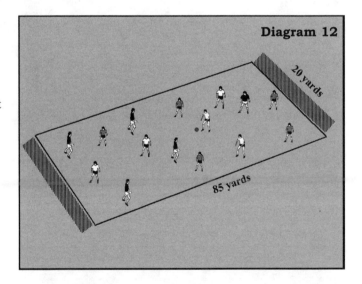

Diagram 12

Progressions

- If the defending team wins possession, they can attempt to score in either end zone before becoming part of the ten-man team
- The two combined teams of ten must pass to each team alternately - for example, a white player must pass to a gray player who must then pass to a white player, etc.
- Play one touch

USYSA National Champions

Contributed by Mike Matkovic the director of coaching for the Chicago Magic Soccer Club. Mike is a U.S.S.F. National Staff Coach, holds a USSF 'A' License and is the head coach of the USYSA Region Two '83 team.

The Chicago Magic U16 Boys have been Illinois State Cup Champions at U12, U13, U15, and U16. They were Region Two semi-finalist in 1998 and Region Two champions in 1999 which they then followed with the USYSA Snickers National Championship later that same year.

Warm-Up
Mark a half-field with a line extending from the penalty area as shown in diagram 13. Play 7 v 7 keep-away with two neutral players playing for the team in possession. Place balls around the area to keep the game moving. Eight consecutive passes score a point. Play four 3-minute games; unlimited touches, two touch, one touch, finishing with unlimited touches.

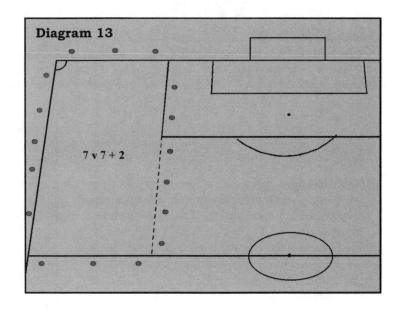

Diagram 13

7 v 7 + 2

Coaching Points
- Tight space increases speed of play
- Pressure the ball and squeeze the area to win possession of the ball - then KEEP IT
- When in possession, draw players toward you then pass into the spaces
- Transition to defense - press quickly
- Transition to offense - spread out

Diagram 14

Four Goal Game
Play from penalty area to penalty area with cones marking two small goals at both sides of the penalty areas. Play 8 v 8 plus two neutral players that play for the team in possession. Usually the two neutral players are our goalkeepers and they are allowed to use their hands. Shape the team in a 3-3-2 formation and have offside in effect. Place balls around the field to keep play moving. Play three 5-minute games - unlimited touches, two touch and unlimited touches.

Coaching Points
- Defensively - stay compact, when to press and when drop off
- Offensively - switch the point of attack, quick play, when to play around v when to get behind
- Transition - where to play the first pass

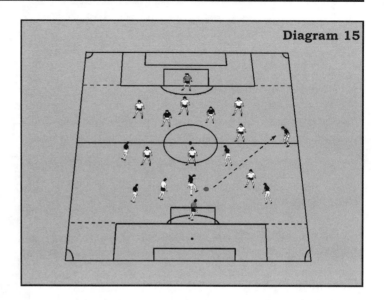

Progression

Progress into using goalkeepers in full size goals on the same size field and playing 8 v 8.

Coaching Points

Now is the time to get across all the previous coaching points in a more realistic game format.

Finishing

Place a goal on the edge of the penalty area and extend lines from the 6-yard box as shown in diagram 16. Play 2 v 2 with unlimited touches inside the area. Position players around the perimeter. The perimeter players can move side to side between the cones but are limited to one touch. Play 2-minute games then rotate the teams.

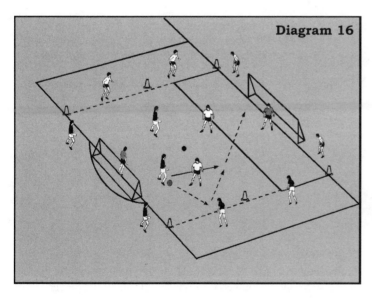

Coaching Points

- Be ready to shoot
- Look for give-and-go's with the perimeter players
- Follow the shots for any rebounds
- Create an attitude to 'finish'
- Do what it takes to score - toe poke, header, etc.

Progression

Allow the perimeter players to shoot.

End practice with a penalty-kick competition followed by a cool down.

Crystal Palace Youth Teams

During my recent visit to England for the FACA Coaches Conference, I had the opportunity to visit the Crystal Palace Youth Academy. There I observed the training sessions of the U11, U15 and U16 teams. The training session was done in the evening, outdoors on an artificial surface. The weather was windy with the temperature close to freezing.

U11 Possession Game
Play 6 v 6 possession in a 30 x 20-yard area. A player is positioned on both of the 30-yard perimeter lines. The players inside the grid can pass to the perimeter players if they wish. The perimeter players can move along their line looking to receive a pass and play the ball back into the grid but they must avoid taking too long to make the pass.

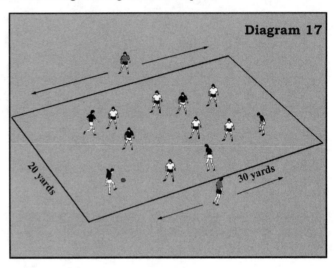

Diagram 17

Progressions
- Perimeter player can dribble the ball in and change places with the player that passed to him
- Play directional

Coaching Point
When the inside player receives a pass from the perimeter player, he should look to open up and see if he can turn.

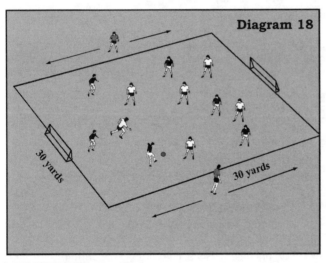

Diagram 18

Progression
Increase the area to 30 x 30 yards and place small goals, cones or flags at both ends. This time the players are playing directional and attempting to score.

Coaching Point
Look to switch play

Practice ended with a 30-minute scrimmage.

U15/U16 Warm-Up
Both teams practiced together. The warm-up was done in a 40 x 40-yard area. Eighteen players, six with balls, moved around inside the grid passing and moving. After a few minutes they stretched then continued with passing and moving, this time looking for give-and-go's. This was done for another few minutes followed by stretches. Then all the players had a ball each and dribbled around inside the grid practicing various fakes and moves. The total time of the warm-up was 15 minutes.

Observations
- Most of the players had arrived 15 - 30 minutes prior to the start of their practice. They practiced ball juggling, etc. waiting for the U11 and U12 teams to finish their training sessions.
- Some of the U11 and U12 players stayed behind when their practice had ended and continued to play 1 v 1 or shoot against a wall while the older boys warmed up despite the extremely cold weather. Only after a few requests did they reluctantly leave when the older boys needed the space to practice.
- The coaches spent time at the end of practice to talk individually with the players and parents.

Crystal Palace Youth Teams

Relay Race

The players were split into three teams. Each team had players 40 yards apart as shown in diagram 19. The first player in line runs with the ball toward the player in the opposite line and touches it a minimum of four times before he passes to his teammate who continues the drill by running in the opposite direction. The first team to complete six cycles (each player making six runs) is the winner.

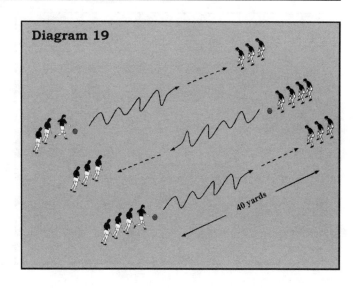

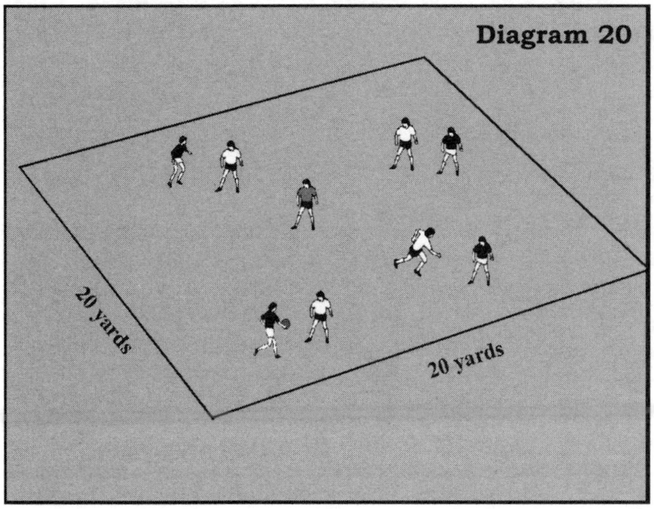

Diagram 19

Hand Ball Game

The coach used this game to get across defensive coaching points. The game was played in 20 x 20-yard area with two teams of four playing keep-away plus one neutral player. The ball was carried in the player's hands and they were allowed to run with the ball or pass it to teammates to avoid getting stripped of the ball. It was similar to basketball except the players didn't have to dribble the ball when they moved. The team not in possession tried to steal the ball or intercept a pass but were not allowed any real physical contact. To receive a pass from a teammate, players had to work hard to get open and find space. If the ball hit the ground, possession went to the other team.

Diagram 20

Coaching Points

The coach stressed many individual defensive points

Progression

The game was progressed by adding cones to form two small goals as shown in diagram 21. To score a goal, players had to throw the ball in the air for themselves to head through the cones. Players could block the goal by swatting the ball away from the player as he is heading toward goal.

Progression

Each player pairs off with someone on the other team. Players can only steal the ball from their partner.

Progression

Now play with feet - be patient, players will make mistakes when playing at speed.

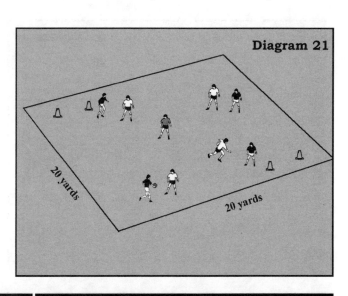

Diagram 21

Crystal Palace Youth Teams

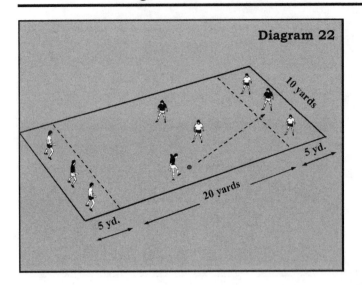

2 v 1 End Zone Game

Mark a 20 x 10-yard area plus 5-yard end zones. In the 20 x 10-yard grid, play two darks v one white. In the end zones, have one dark player and two white players. The objective is for the two dark players inside the grid to pass to their teammate in either end zone who controls and then passes back. Change players every few minutes.

Progression

Play 3 v 2 inside the grid with one white player and one dark player in each end zone. Again, the objective is to pass the ball to a teammate in the end zone. This time however, when his teammate receives the ball, his objective is to attempt to turn and take the ball over the end-line of the end zone under control while being defended by the white player in the end zone. If the defender blocks the turn he can pass back inside the grid and play continues.

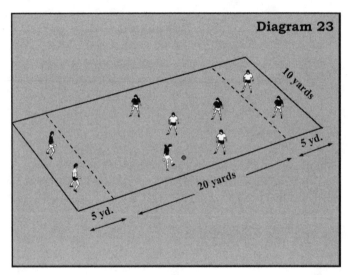

Small-Sided Possession Game

The players then play 5 v 5 keep-away in a 40 x 30-yard grid. Five consecutive passes score a point.

Four Goal Game

Play 5 v 5 in a 25 x 25-yard grid with four small goals as shown in diagram 24, with each team defending two goals.

Practice ended with both teams combining to play a 9 v 9 scrimmage on a half-field for the last 30 minutes.

Bob Gansler

Now the Head Coach of the Kansas City Wizards, Bob Gansler has a wealth of coaching experience including coaching the U.S. National Team in the 1990 World Cup Finals. This session is aimed at developing a good first touch for youth players. The session was part of the KSYSA workshop and was conducted with the Kansas 86 Boys ODP team. The entire session was done indoors in a 20 x 30-yard area (obviously a larger area would be used when working outdoors) and consisted of a number of warm-up exercises and small-sided games.

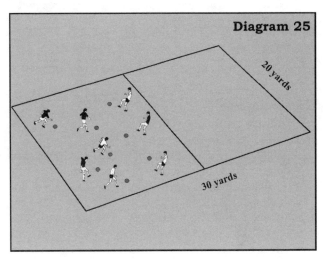

Diagram 25

Warm-Up

Two teams of four players dribble the ball in one half of the field. After every 30 seconds the coach gives them a signal to move to the other half of the field. The coach also gives the players certain conditions such as dribbling using only the left foot, only the right foot or alternating each touch with the left and right feet, etc.

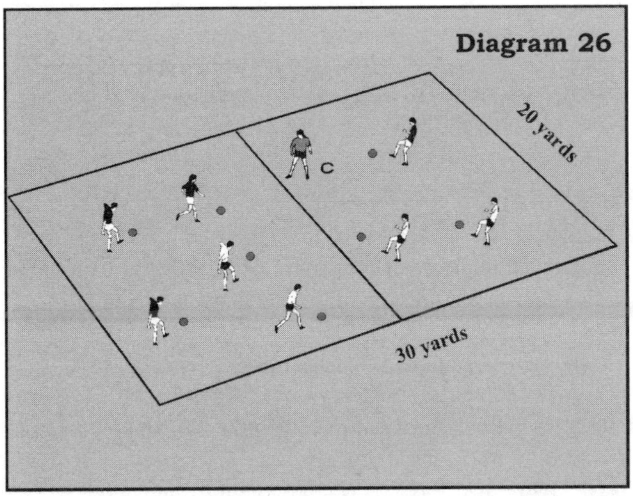

Diagram 26

Warm-Up

All eight players juggle the ball allowing a bounce after every touch. The coach moves around the field and the players follow him while juggling.

Coaching Points

- Have a compact body position over the ball - don't stretch
- Give the players instructions of sequences: left foot, right foot, left thigh, etc. This is important as they learn to control where the ball should go instead of just reacting to where the ball goes.

Warm-Up

In pairs three yards apart, one player serves the ball from his hands to his partner's thigh. The partner controls with his thigh and volleys it back with the inside of his foot. Change servers after every few attempts. Vary the sequences to include chest and head as well as thighs and feet.

Coaching Points

- 'Dance' - always be on your toes
- Agility - the standing foot should not be planted but should be able to move to enable any necessary adjustments

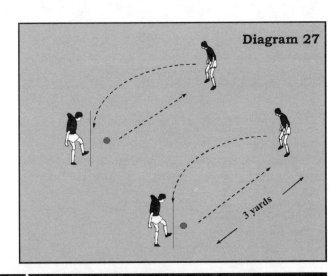

Diagram 27

Bob Gansler

Three v One

Play 3 v 1 in each half. The player responsible for losing possession alternates positions with the defender. However, the defender MUST win the ball. If the defender kicks the ball out-of-bounds then play is restarted with the three players retaining possession. Play games of one touch, two touch and three touch. The players must use the required number of touches, i.e., if playing three touch, the players must use three touches and can't pass the ball in fewer touches. Also, play a game where the players can use one touch or three touches but not two touches. Another option is to require multiple touches with the same foot, i.e., receive with the right foot and pass with the right foot.

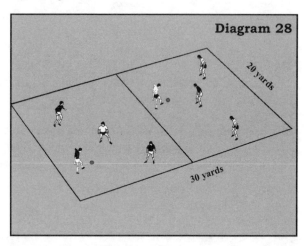

Diagram 28

Coaching Points

- Don't stop the ball - keep it moving
- Disguise your controlling touch and passes
- Asking the players to use only the stated number of touches requires them to think about what they are doing
- Pass with the outside of your foot - it is quicker and more deceptive

Two v Two v Two Keep-Away

Organize three pairs of players in different colored jerseys. In diagram 29, the dark and gray players combine to play keep-away from the white players. The team responsible for losing possession alternates with the white players and become defenders.

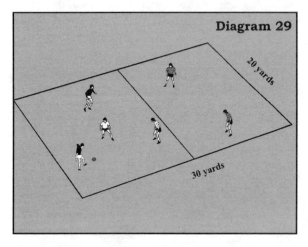

Diagram 29

Coaching Points

- Quick transition
- Use the inside and outside of the foot to control the ball and keep it moving - using the sole of the foot slows the ball movement
- Look for the penetrating pass that splits the defenders - it is usually a one-touch pass
- Get your body in position when receiving the ball so you can see all your options
- Kicking the ball out-of-bounds is not enough for the defenders to change places - they must win the ball

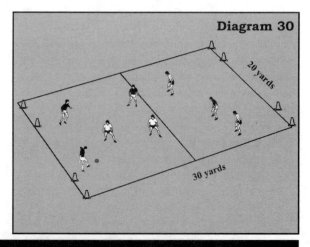

Diagram 30

Small-Sided Game

Play 4 v 4 with each team defending two small goals as shown in diagram 30.

Variations

- The defending team has one player kneeling
- The attacking team has one player kneeling

Coaching Points

- Play two touch or three touch
- Look for the penetrating pass

Manchester United - U17 & U19

In December 1999 I spent the morning at Manchester United with David Williams, the coach of the Manchester United U19 team. It was a few days before the Christmas break with some players already home for the holidays, so the U17 and U19 teams combined for this training session. The temperature was about 38 degrees with 10-20 mph winds. On arriving at the field, the players quickly got themselves into two groups of nine and played one touch keep-away in a small 5-yard area.

Warm-Up

Neil Bailey, the U17's coach, conducted the warm-up while David Williams did the goalkeeper warm-up. Neil Bailey took the players on a 12-minute run followed by five minutes of stretches. The field players then did a series of sprints over a 20-yard distance then jogged back to the starting line. This consisted of many variations of sprints such as high knees, side-steps, short quick steps, long strides, etc.

Organize nine players in each half of a 70 x 45-yard area with three balls in each half. The players pass and move staying in their own half doing the following techniques. Each technique was done for two minutes followed by two minutes of stretching.

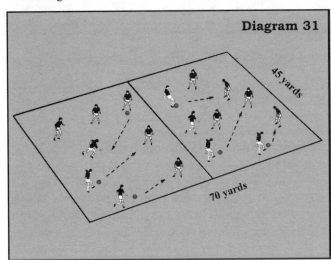

Diagram 31

- Receive with the inside of the foot and immediately move away pushing the ball with the outside of the same foot.
- Receive using the same technique as above but this time use softer passes and sprint away for 5-10 yards after receiving the ball.
- Control with an open body position and move away.
- Control with the outside of the foot and move away.
- Firm passes, short and long, as required in a game situation - receive using a variety of the previous techniques

Two v Two v Two Keep-Away

Organize into three groups of six players with each group having three pairs in different colored jerseys. Mark a 60 x 20-yard area into three 20 x 20-yard areas. Each group plays 4 v 2 keep-away with two pairs combining to play against the other pair. Play for one minute then change the defenders. Play three games so each pair has a turn at defending. Then play another three games using two touches followed by another three games where three attackers are limited to one touch and the other attacker has unlimited touches.

Coaching Points

- Use the receiving techniques practiced in the warm-up
- Defenders to work extremely hard
- The pressing defender might not win the ball but he can affect where it goes
- The pressing defender should clearly force the ball in one direction so his partner knows where the ball is going
- Defenders should work for each other

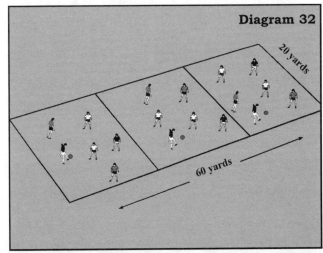

Diagram 32

3/4 Field Game

Organize the players into two teams of nine players using a 4-3-2 formation. Play two 20-minute halves. Offside is in effect. Any player that shoots the ball high or wide of the goal has to go and collect it while the game continues without him. This made them think hard about shooting on target as their team plays a player short while he was collecting the ball.

Editors note: *For this training session, only one goalkeeper was present. Therefore, the game was adapted slightly by having one team defend a small goal without a goalkeeper. The attacking team could only score in this goal with a one-touch finish*

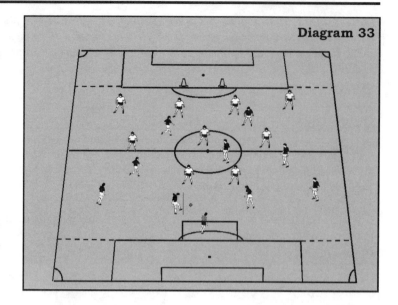

Diagram 33

Observations

• The players worked extremely hard throughout the entire training session
• Even though the temperature was barely above freezing, all the players wore shorts.
• During the warm-up, the players really focused on the techniques they were practicing
• All the exercises and the game were played at an extremely quick (game-like) pace
• During the game, David Williams talked to the players about taking responsibility by wanting and asking for the ball from teammates
• The game got extremely competitive toward the end

Norwich City F.C.

Contributed by Steve Foley, Reserve Team Manager, Norwich City Football Club of the English First Division. All of the drills come under the title "I know you have a left and a right foot - but have you got a front and a back foot?"

The practice starts with some basic circle work to allow the players to get plenty of touches. You can use your imagination with circle drills and there are literally hundreds of different levels to reach depending on the quality of your players. I have made these drills basic so they can be used with any level of player. The coach should progress the drills as he sees fit. He should always try to ask questions of his players to test their ability.

If you are in doubt, the work areas should be big to start and as the players begin to progress and feel more comfortable you can make the area smaller and introduce conditions such as two-touch, one-touch, etc.

The modern soccer game is condensed into small areas of the field. Players can get out of tight situations by being 'side on'. These drills will give them the confidence to do so.

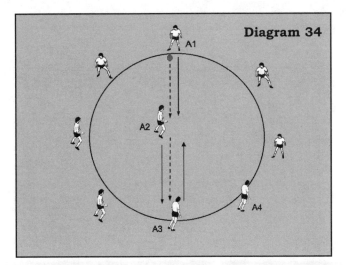

Exercise One
A1 plays the ball into A2 and follows his pass.
A2 receives the ball (side on) on his 'back foot', then passes to A3 and follows his pass.
A3 passes to A1 and continues the rotation.

Coaching Point
When receiving the ball, your shoulders should be parallel to the line of the pass - side on.

Exercise Two
A1 plays a pass to A2 and follows his pass.
A2 receives the ball (side on) on his 'back foot', then passes to A3 and follows his pass.
A3 receives the pass (side on) on his 'back foot' and passes to A4 and follows his pass.
A4 passes to A1 and continues the rotation.

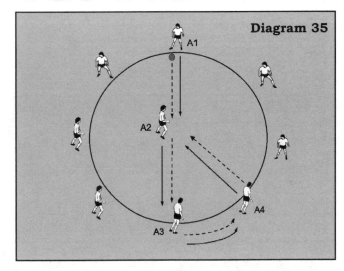

Norwich City F.C.

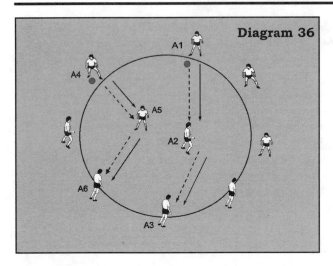

Diagram 36

Exercise Three
Same as Exercise Two but with two balls.
A1 and A4 begin the movement, making sure they pass, follow and receive the 'same' ball.

Coaching Points
- Quality of pass
- Body shape (side on) to receive ball
- Head movement
- Movement of players
- Start with unlimited touches then progress to two-touch

Exercise Four
Organize the players into a diamond shape.
A1 passes to A2 and follows his pass.
A2 checks away (to lose an imaginary defender) before receiving the ball 'side on'.
Then A2 has a decision to make:
  A. If it's a hard pass, play two-touch.
  B. If it's a soft pass, let it run, go to meet it, or play it around the corner (hook).
Continue to A3.
The pass should always be played on the outside of the cones (defenders), if possible. Speed up practice with less touches.

Coaching Points
- Movement of player before receiving
- Head movement - awareness
- Body shape when receiving
- Decision - let it run across your body or play it around corners
- Quality of pass, stress pace and quality

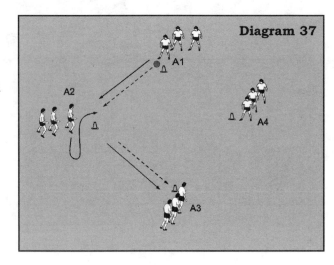

Diagram 37

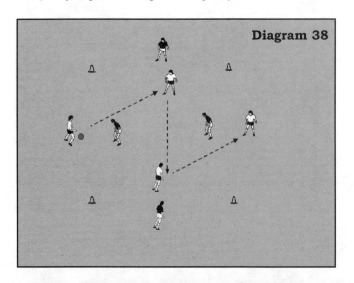

Diagram 38

Exercise Five
Organize two teams of four players. Play 2 v 2 inside the grid with the other four players on the perimeter. The players on the outside are restricted to two touches and cannot go inside the grid. The players inside the grid play unlimited touches.

Coaching Points
- The players in possession should stay wide, receive side on, play around corners, let the ball run, etc.
- No tackling from outside players
- Short bursts, then rotate inside and outside players

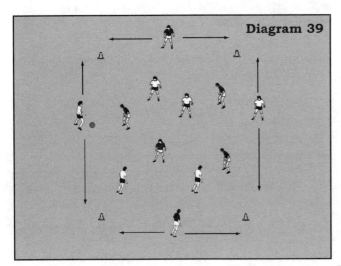

Diagram 39

Exercise Six

End the session with a game. Organize two teams of six players. Play 4 v 4 keep-away inside the grid using the two players from each team on the perimeter. One team plays across the field, one team plays up and down.

Coaching Points
• Movement to lose defenders
• Body shape to receive ball
• Decisions
• Give-and-go's, around corners, etc.

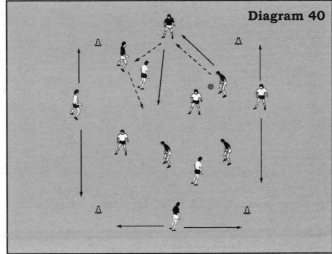

Diagram 40

Progression

Perimeter players can alternate positions with their teammates inside the grid.

U.S. U18 Women's National Team

Contributed by Jeff Pill, U.S. Women's National Staff Coach and U.S. Women's U18 National Team Assistant Coach.
You can find more of Jeff's training sessions at www.eteamz.com/soccer/pills/jpill.htm

During a recent camp with the U.S. Women's U18 National Team held at the ARCO Olympic Training Center in Chula Vista, CA, the team spent a week together in preparation for their upcoming trip to Bulgaria.

We found that several areas needed to be addressed. They were:
1. *The coordination of the defending action of the back four and midfield four.*
2. *The coordination of the defending action of the midfielders and strikers.*
3. *Being able to consistently play into the strikers and create opportunities from those penetrating passes.*

The following three activities addressed those problems effectively. They are the activities that we used during the course of the week as part of a bigger progression. However, they all were the major teaching activity that was used to assist the players as they learned their roles within the team.

We were finding it difficult to play into our strikers once we won the ball, and, if we did get it to them, we had difficulty creating opportunities to get to goal. This activity addressed that concern and improved their play. It is a good functional game for both sides of the ball because it also works on the two strikers defending play out of the back, and the center backs.

Activity One
The three light players in Zone 'A' keep the ball away from the two dark players and try to pass the ball over the line to the two light players in Zone 'B'. The three dark players in zone 'B' must mark from behind. If the dark team wins the ball, it is their turn to attack.

Stages
1. Light players play keep-away from dark players. They may only pass the ball back and forth over the line. Everyone must stay in their zones.
2. Same game as above, but one player can 'move up' to support when the ball is played in (e.g.: Zone 'A' player can follow his pass into Zone 'B').
3. Same as above, but the two players in Zone 'B' must combine before they can pass to a different player.
4. Play to goal. (Goalkeepers may be added at any time in this sequence.) The game is free flowing and restarted properly if the ball goes out-of-bounds.

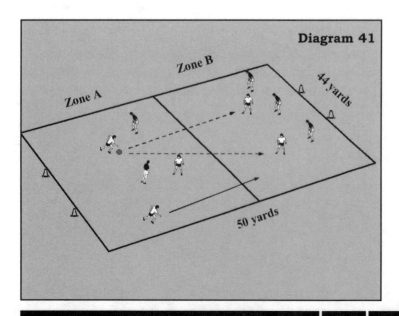

Diagram 41

Zone B

Zone A

44 yards

50 yards

Coaching Points
- Keep the ball by playing it back or sideways, but play it forward whenever possible
- The best pass is always the longest pass as long as possession can be maintained
- Anticipate 'windows of opportunity' in order to play the ball forward
- Look for the 'second forward'
- Pace of passes must be appropriate.
- 'Checking forward' must read the defender (turn, hold, or combine)
- Angle, distance and timing of support
- Back players try to combine with 'strikers'
- Forwards try to get behind defenders once the ball is played back - always 'spin' after laying the ball back

U.S. U18 Women's National Team

We needed to improve the team's ability to coordinate the defense of the back four and midfield four. Too many gaps were present, and, they had difficulty reading how, when, and where to put pressure on the ball. This activity addressed that concern well. It also gave the team confidence in the defending 'system' as this game showed them that they could play numbers down and still have success with their defending.

Activity Two

The 'white team' attacks with all 11 players.
The 'dark team' can only defend with eight field players and a keeper.
If the 'dark team' wins the ball, the two strikers, who are waiting outside the marked line, can come back in to their own half and assist the team in getting the ball over the marked line.
Once this is done, the game is now reversed, with the 'darks' attacking against the 'lights' nine players (the two light strikers go and wait in their attacking half beyond their marked line).

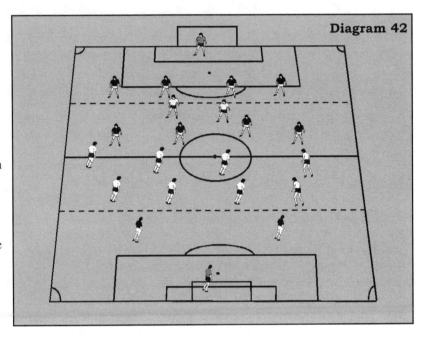

Diagram 42

Coaching Points

- Good communication from ALL members of the defending team
- Stay compact. Keep gaps tight to make it difficult for the attacking team to play
- Good individual defending - don't lunge in
- Weak side defenders need to pinch in and help
- Keep the lines of defense clear
- Midfield defenders must stay in midfield and not get sucked back in to the defensive line
- If the attacking team loses the ball, they apply pressure immediately to try to take advantage of their brief numerical superiority

Activity Three

To help improve the coordinated defensive action of our front players with our midfielders, we played this activity.
Early on, our strikers had the tendency to charge after the ball, opening up a big gap between them and the midfielders. As a result, their backs played the ball easily around us and were able to penetrate into our half.

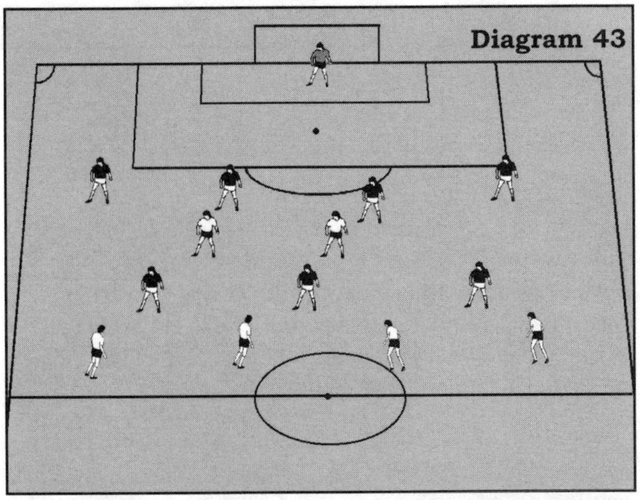

Diagram 43

The Game

6 v 7 plus a keeper.
The seven 'dark' players score a goal by dribbling over the half line.
The six 'light' players score by shooting in to the big goal.

Lausanne - Switzerland

Contributed by coach Adrian Ursea of the Switzerland Division One club, Lausanne.

Today, soccer is considered a 'situational' sport throughout every minute of the game. Because of that fact, the players have to be coached to be able to adjust, and apply 'situational' responses throughout the match. I call this a correlation between risk and advantages. In the game, the player has to put into practice all his technical and tactical abilities in order to tilt the balance towards his advantage. In order to do that, he has to constantly consider the following factors:

- Perception
- Analysis
- Decision
- Action (pass, shot, dribbling, etc.)

Based on the above, I propose practice sessions based on games (different objectives) where the players meet these 'situational' moments in the presence of active opponents.

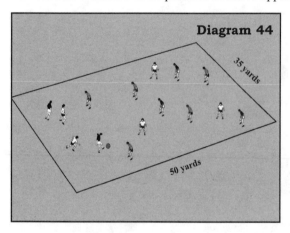

Diagram 44

35 yards

50 yards

Warm-Up

Organize three teams of five in a 50 x 35-yard area. Each team wears a different colored jersey. Two teams combine to play keep-away from the other team making it 10 v 5. The team that is responsible for losing possession becomes the defending team. Play unlimited touches to start then reduce the number of touches allowed.

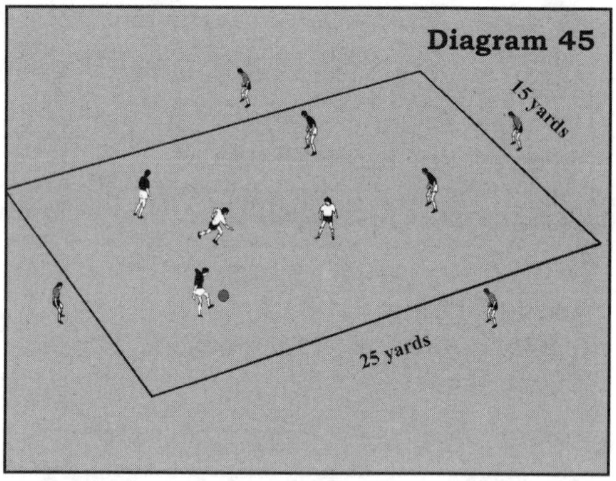

Small-Sided Game

On a field 25 x 15 yards, play 4 v 2 keep-away with four players on the perimeter. The players inside the grid have unlimited touches, the perimeter players are limited to one touch. The game should be played at a fast pace. Every two minutes the team of two should alternate with two perimeter players. Progress to two-touch by the inside players later in the session.

Progression

Play 4 v 3 and when an inside player passes to a perimeter player they alternate positions.

Diagram 45

15 yards

25 yards

Diagram 46

30 yards

40 yards

Small-Sided Game To One Goal

Mark a field 40 x 30 yards with a full size goal and goalkeeper. Play 4 v 4 with three perimeter players as shown. The objective is for either team to score after having possession but only if they have passed to a perimeter player during their possession. Start by playing unlimited touches then reduce the number of touches later in the session.

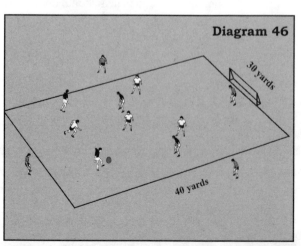

Tampa Bay Mutiny

Observed in Florida, February 2000, during pre-season training.

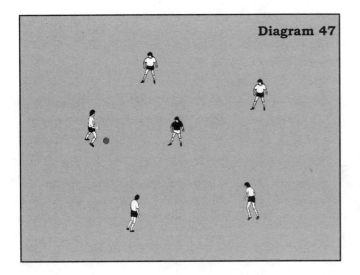

Diagram 47

Warm-up

The players started off with an informal warm-up in groups of 5 or 6 playing keep-away. This was followed by a team warm-up of jogging and stretching that lasted for almost 30 minutes.

Seven Goals Game

On a field 45 x 25 yards, place seven small goals using cones or flags. Play 9 v 9 with the players having unlimited touches. Goals are scored by passing the ball through any of the small goals to a teammate who must maintain control of the ball when he receives it. The first team to score 10 goals wins.

Progression

- Play two-touch to five goals
- Play one-touch to two goals - add a neutral player who plays for the team in possession

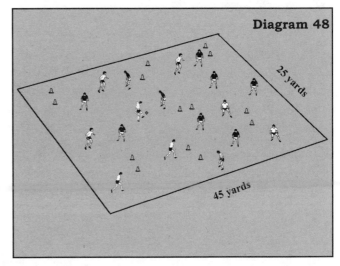

Diagram 48

25 yards

45 yards

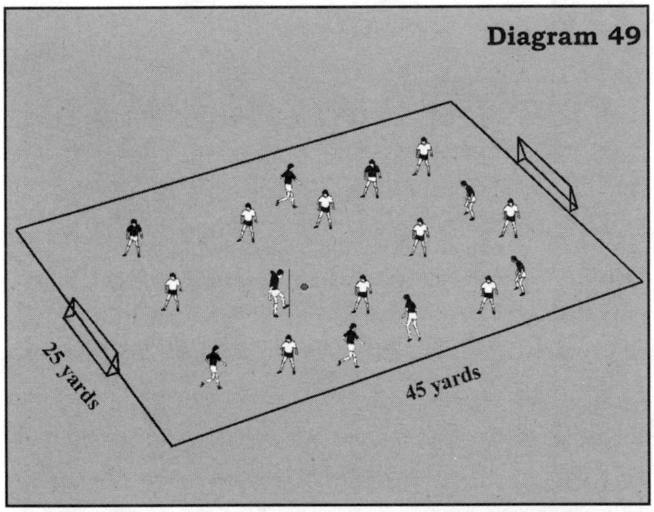

Diagram 49

25 yards

45 yards

Small-Sided Game

Using the same 25 x 45-yard area, place two small goals at each end (cones or flags could be used). On the goal-line of each goal, place two flat disc cones and place a ball on each disc cone. To score a goal, a ball must be knocked off it's cone. Play 9 v 9 + 1 one-touch for 12 minutes.

Nepal National Team

Contributed by Stephen Constantine, Head Coach of the Nepal National Team. Stephen is the holder of both the USSF and UEFA 'A' Licenses. After three years coaching in the U.S., Stephen, a native of England, moved to Cyprus where he coached at professional clubs, Ahilleas F.C., Ael F.C. and Apep F.C. of the Cyprus First Division, where he was the head coach. In July 1998 Constantine was invited to join the England Under 18 National Team coaching staff at the UEFA Championships where England qualified for the World Cup in Nigeria with responsibilities for scouting. In August 1999 he was appointed as the head coach of the Nepal National Team.

On arriving in Nepal, the first thing that struck me is their love for the game. Here soccer is the number one sport everyone wants to play. The Nepalese players are some of the most coachable I have had the pleasure to work with, always trying to improve their game.

The facilities for the National Team are good. We have a complex that can house up to 60 players at any one time, with training facilities on site. One of the main difficulties is the lack of financial resources as limited sponsorship is a major problem. Another problem is the poverty and the fact that some people don't have their most basic needs met. This is a shock to many Westerners who are used to life with modern conveniences. Having said that, the people here always have a smile on their face and are only too happy to help if they can.

Warm-Up
In groups of 6 - 8 players, keep the ball in the air using no more than two touches. If the ball hits the ground, the last player to touch it does 10 sit ups. This encourages players to put their teammates under pressure with difficult to deal with passes. We would probably do this exercise for 10-15 minutes.

Session One
As shown in diagram 50, set up two cones five yards apart for the players to pass through and place five markers/cones on either side three yards apart for the players to run through.
Players in groups of 6 - 8 form two lines either side of the cones in a central position.
Player one passes the ball through the cones to the opposite player about five yards through the other side of the cones and then runs to his right and zigzags through markers, after which he joins the opposite line.
Player two returns the pass to player three and runs to his right to zigzag through the markers to continue the sequence.

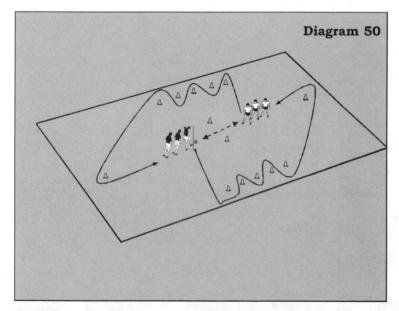

Diagram 50

Variations
- Make the distance between players longer than five yards
- Make the distance smaller so they head or juggle the ball and then go off to the markers before joining the back of the line
- Have the players go up around and back, side to side, or just run straight past the markers
- Increase the distance between the markers

Nepal National Team

Session Two

The number of players you have available would determine the size of the field. We usually go with 8 v 8 v 8 on a full field. The white team starts by attacking the goal defended by the dark team. As soon as the white team crosses the half-line, the dark team can leave the six-yard box to pressure the attacking team. If the white team scores, they then take ball and attack the opposite goal defended by the grey team. The team that concedes a goal does 25 sit-ups.

If the defending team wins the ball and crosses the half-line, either with a pass or a dribble, the attacking team sprints to their own six-yard box and waits for the next attack to cross over the half-line. While resting, we encourage them to stretch. This game incorporates all aspects of the game. It has proved a great favorite with all the teams I have coached. It is important that all teams have a goalkeeper as this makes it more realistic. This would be played for 20-30 minutes as it is high intensity. A good 15-20 minutes cool down would follow.

Variation

A variation of this could be having portable goals placed on the 18-yard line with 5-6 players.

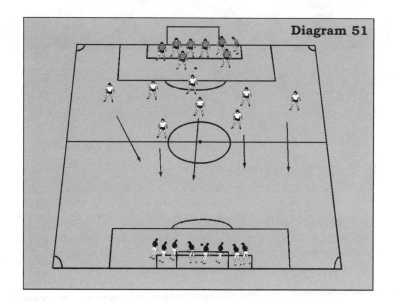

Diagram 51

Training U14 Girls

Contributed by Jeff Pill, U.S. Women's National Staff Coach, U.S. Women's U18 National Team Assistant Coach and U14 Region One Director of Coaching. The following practices are part of the curriculum of the Region One U14 Girls ODP camp. You can find more of Jeff's training sessions at www.eteamz.com/soccer/pills/jpill.htm

This practice focuses on passing, receiving and possession. The following are the coaching points for the entire session:

Passing - use various surfaces - instep, inside and outside of foot, etc.

Receiving - get in the line of flight, be first to the ball, make early decisions, keep the ball outside your immediate space

Team Shape - support, decisions of first and second attackers, change the point of attack

Possession - pass with a purpose

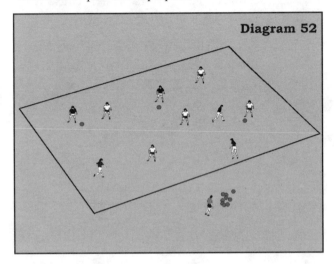

Diagram 52

Three Ball Keep-Away

The size of the area will vary depending on the number of players. In this example there are two teams of five and three balls. The objective is for one team to have possession of two of the three balls at any given time.

4 v 4 v 4 Middle Zone Game

Organize three teams of four in a 50 x 30-yard area with a 10-yard middle zone as shown in diagram 53. The dark team has four players in one end zone and the white team has four players in the other end zone. The objective is for the dark and white teams to keep the ball away from the grey team. This can be done by passing to their own players or passing long into the other end zone. The grey team can send only two players into an end zone at one time. The two other grey players must remain in the middle zone. The grey team can get out of the middle by replacing the team that loses the ball out-of-bounds or by stealing it from one team and passing to the other team in the opposite end zone.

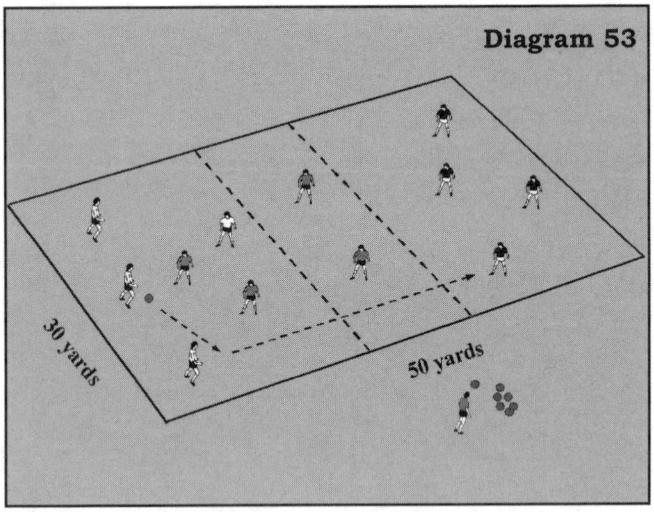

Diagram 53

30 yards

50 yards

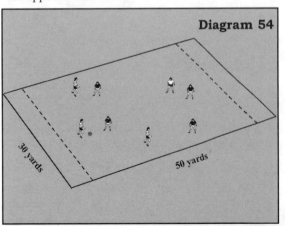

Diagram 54

30 yards

50 yards

End Zone Game

Play 4 v 4 on a 50 x 30-yard field with 5-yard end zones as shown in diagram 54. The objective is for the attacking team to attack one end zone. If the defending team wins the ball, they can attack either end zone. Players are not allowed to defend inside the end zones.

End practice with a conditioned game focusing on correct technique, team shape and possession/penetration decisions.

Training U14 Girls

This practice is a technical/tactical session focusing on dribbling for possession or to beat an opponent. The following are the coaching points for the entire session:
- Change of speed and direction
- Correct "side-on" shielding technique
- Have two or three moves you are comfortable with to beat an opponent
- Have a mind set to attack your opponent

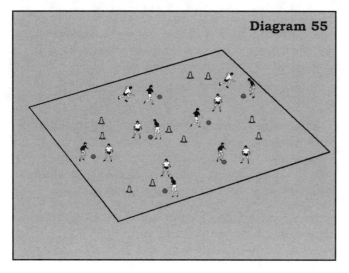

Diagram 55

Multi-Goal Game
Organize the players in pairs with a ball for each pair. One team attacks, the other team defends. Set up cones to make small goals as shown in diagram 55. Have two less goals than number of defenders. The objective is for the attacking players to score by dribbling through any of the goals. However, they can't score through the same goal twice in a row. Switch teams after an interval.

Four Goal Circle Game
Place cones to make four small goals in a circle as shown in diagram 56. Organize the players into three pairs with a ball for each pair. Whoever has the ball attacks. The objective is for the player with the ball to score in any of the goals. Goals can only be scored from the inside of the circle. Keep score to make the game competitive.

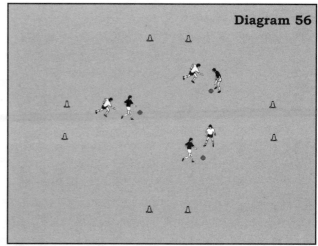

Diagram 56

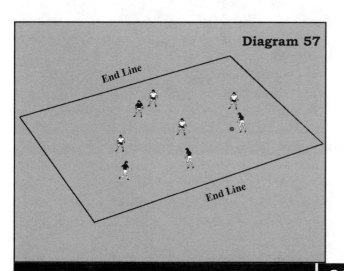

Diagram 57

End Line

End Line

4 v 4 Line Game
Play 4 v 4 on a short wide field. The objective of the game is to score a goal by dribbling over the opposition's line.

End practice with a conditioned game with an emphasis on dribbling technique, decisions of when to dribble and team shape.

FC Petrolul Ploiesti

Contributed by FC Petrolul Ploiesti head coach Nicolae Lazar. FC Petrolul Ploiesti plays in Division One of the Romanian Football League. This practice is designed to improve the transition from the defensive third of the field to the attacking third in the quickest time possible.

The following are some of my thoughts regarding advancing the ball into the attacking third of the field as quickly as possible.

• As a rule, attackers in advanced positions must be the fastest on the team, constantly on the move, always trying to run into open spaces and repositioning themselves in order to be able to rid themselves of the defenders marking them.

• Passes between the forwards should be quick and firm.

• Long forward passes should be flighted so that the ball lands behind the defenders in the running path of the forwards who will take it to the goal.

• If the ball is too short, the forwards first have to battle for possession of the ball and if they are successful, only then be able to pick up speed and try to score. In real game situations, the most effective passes are lobbed balls, which most likely will beat defenders coming out for an interception.

• Lobbed or long diagonal passes can also create open spaces for the wingers because they can run onto the ball without turning or stopping. When the pass is quick and unexpected, usually the wingers will not be troubled to receive the ball because the defenders are positioned mainly along the trajectory of the ball.

• If the forwards succeed in running onto a pass into an open space, they should strike towards the goal along the shortest route in the quickest time. The attack is most effective when his partner stays close to the player with the ball and is available for a pass or a rebound.

• These practice games are also valuable for the defenders dealing with these type of attacks.

Small-Sided Games

The following practice games could be played on small fields, across a half-field, in two-thirds of the field, or on a full size field. Any number from 8 - 22 players can participate in these type of practices.

2 v 2

Play across a half-field between the 18-yard line and the half-line. Mark a 15-yard wide area in the middle of the field separating the two end zones. Organize two groups of 2 v 2 in each end zone. The dark team defends one end-line and the white team defends the other end-line. The objective is to pass the ball to a teammate in the attacking zone who then attempts to score by dribbling the ball across the end-line himself or by passing to his other teammate in the attacking zone.

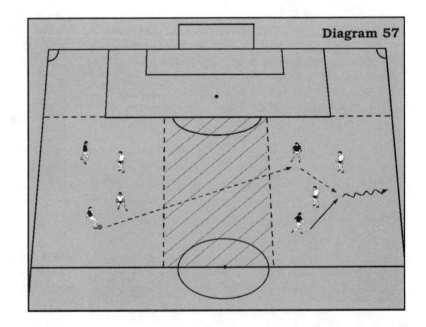

Diagram 57

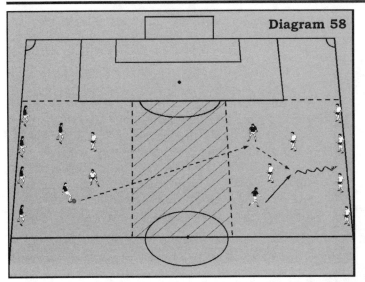

Diagram 58

Variations

- Add four players for each team who now defend each end-line as shown in diagram 58. A goal can be scored by passing or shooting the ball over the end-line below knee height.

- Score by shooting into a small goal on each end-line (no goalkeepers).

- Score by shooting into a full-size goal with goalkeepers.

3 v 2 Half-Field

The objective of this practice is the same as the previous 2 v 2 practice. This time the entire half of the field is used. Play 3 v 2 in each end zone. Instead of dribbling over the end-line to score, they now have to shoot below knee height into 20-yard wide goals marked by cones and defended by a goalkeeper. This game is fast paced and physically demanding so the players rotate every five minutes.

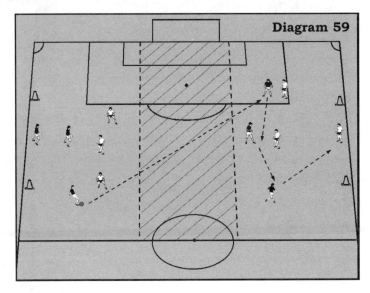

Diagram 59

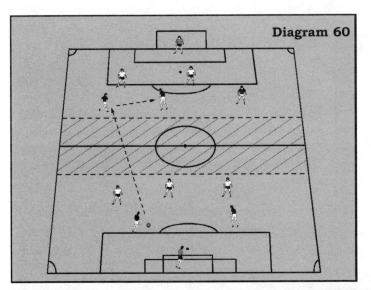

Diagram 60

3 v 2 Full-Field

The same exercise as in diagram 60, except use the full field with a 20-yard area separating the two end zones and attack full-size goals with goalkeepers.

AFC Manawatu - New Zealand

Contributed by Richard Hudson, head coach of the New Zealand First Division team, AFC Manawatu. This article focuses on passing and possession.

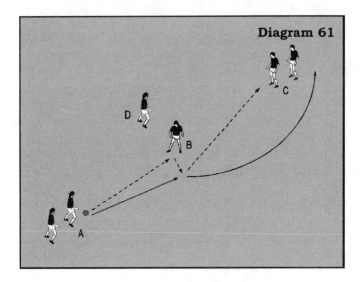

Diagram 61

Passing Warm-Up

This is a straight forward passing drill. The distance can be altered for short or long passes. The drill starts with player A passing to player B who lays off a one-touch pass for incoming player A. Player A passes to player C and follows his pass to the end of the opposite line. Player C continues the drill by passing to player D. Rotate the center players every few minutes.

Coaching Points
- Crisp firm passes
- Change of pace following your pass
- Quality one-touch lay-off

Progression

The same organization as diagram 62 with the addition of one more player in the center. The drill starts with player A passing to player B who lays a one-touch pass back to player A. Player A then plays a give-and-go with player C and passes to player D. Player D continues the drill in the opposite direction using player E. Player A joins the back of the opposite line. Rotate the center players every few minutes.

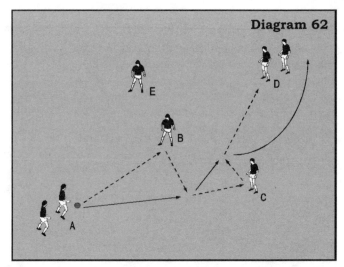

Diagram 62

Diagram 63

Passing Rotations

Organize six players in a 40 x 20-yard area as shown in diagram 63. Player A1 starts the drill by passing to B1. B1 passes to B2.
B2 hits an aerial pass to A2 who lays a one-touch pass to A1.
A1 hits an aerial pass to C1.
C1 continues the drill by hitting an aerial pass to A1.
Rotate positions every few minutes.

Coaching Points - Diagram 35
- The quality of the aerial passes are critical for the drill to be successful
- The receiving player should adjust his position to get in line with the flight of the ball
- The receiving touch should set you up for your next pass
- When A2 is receiving the aerial pass from B2, A1 should adjust his position while the ball is in the air in terms of supporting A2 at the correct angle and distance

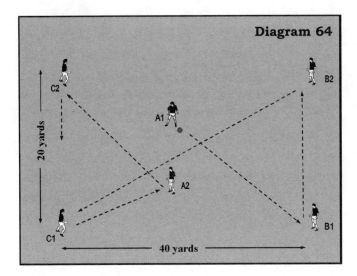

Diagram 64

Passing Rotations
Use the same organization as diagram 64 except this time player B2 drives a long diagonal pass to the player at the opposite corner, C1.
C1 lays a one-touch pass to A2 who passes to C2.
C2 passes to C1.
C1 drives a long diagonal pass and the drill continues.
Rotate the players every few minutes.

Progressions
- Use one-touch passes whenever possible
- Give the players the choice to play aerial passes to the center players or driven passes to the opposite diagonal corners

Coaching Points - Diagram 64
- The quality of the driven passes are critical for the drill to be successful
- The receiving player should adjust his position to get in line with the flight of the ball and control the ball to the side of his body in which he will make his next pass
- Encourage a body feint before receiving a pass
- The receiving touch should set you up for your next pass
- When C1 is receiving the driven pass from B2, A2 should adjust his position before C1 receives the pass in terms of supporting C2 at the correct angle and distance

4 v 2 Zone Game
Organize a 60 x 20-yard area marked into three 20-yard zones as shown in diagram 65. Four players are positioned in each zone. The coach starts by passing the ball into Zone A. As soon as one of the four players in that zone has touched the ball, two players from Zone B can enter the zone and attempt to win possession. The objective is for the four players in Zone A to combine passes and then make a long pass to the players in Zone C. As soon as the player in Zone C touches the ball, the other two players from Zone B enter and try to win possession. If the two players from Zone B win possession, all four B players change zones with the team that lost possession.

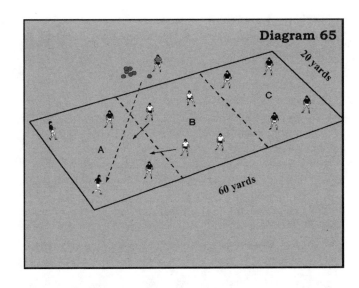

Diagram 65

Coaching Points
- Good support play - angles and distance of support
- Quality of first touch and passes

5 v 2 Passing

Organize three teams of five players in a 40 x 20-yard area as shown in diagram 66. One team is defending from the other two teams who are positioned in each half of the field. The defending team must keep three players on the half-line at all times. The other two players enter the half of the field where the ball is. Each time the ball is played over the half-line, two defenders can leave the half-line to pressure the ball with the other two defenders returning to the half-line. Change the defending team after they have won possession five times or following a pre-determined time limit.

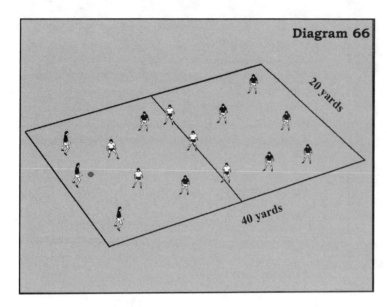

Diagram 66

Game Conditions

- Set a minimum or maximum number of passes before the ball is passed over the half-line
- The three defenders on the half-line can intercept the pass into the opposite half
- Use two-touch

Coaching Points

- Good first touch away from the defender
- Disguise your intentions
- Head-up - awareness
- Selection of pass

Full-Field Game

Organize two teams of eight players (including goalkeepers) on a full-field. Mark the field with lines extending down the field from the sides of the penalty area as shown in diagram 67. This game can be used to get across all the coaching points from the previous drills in a more game-like situation. Special focus can be given to playing out from the defensive third, options and choices of midfielders and various attacking formations.

Coaching Points

- Positioning of defenders when goalkeeper has possession
- Clearance of space by pushing forward of midfielders when goalkeeper has possession
- Distribution of the goalkeeper
- Passing decisions from the defenders - do they pass short to a midfielder or long to a forward
- Midfielders must position themselves for a pass from the defenders or a lay-off from the forwards
- Midfielders decision to run with the ball to exploit space or pass
- Movement by the forwards to receive the ball from defenders or midfielders
- Decisions of the forwards to turn, dribble or pass to a supporting player

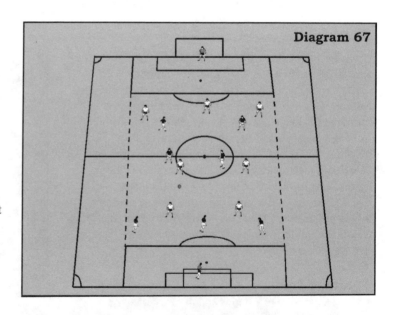

Diagram 67

Nottingham Forest U11 Youth Team

Contributed by Nottingham Forest youth team coach, Peter Cooper. Peter has experience coaching youth players of different ages at a number of English Premier League clubs including Leeds United and now Nottingham Forest. This article focuses on passing and movement both on and off the ball.

Organize the players into two teams of eight with five players from each team forming a circle and the other three players from each team playing 3 v 3 inside the circle. The size of the circle will be determined by the age and ability level of the players. The 3 v 3 players in the center play keep-away from each other. If they are not able to pass to one of their teammates they can pass to any perimeter player. The perimeter players then pass the ball back to the same team they received the pass from.

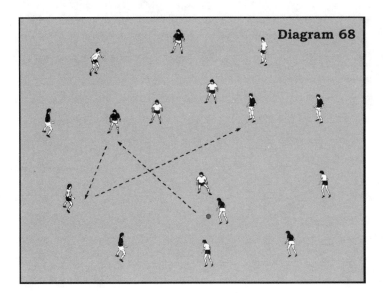

Diagram 68

Coaching Points

- Remind the players that they have a 13 v 3 situation when they have possession
- Don't over complicate things - keep it simple
- Open up your body position when receiving a pass and receive the ball on your back foot so that you can see more of the playing area
- Only use the perimeter players if you can't pass to a teammate

Progression

The players in the center can only use the perimeter players of their own team. The perimeter players have a maximum of two touches and then one touch.

Progression

When a player from the center passes to a perimeter player, he shouts, "Change". The perimeter player then dribbles the ball into the center and looks to pass to one of his teammates. The center player takes the position of the incoming perimeter player.

Coaching Point

The perimeter player entering the inside of the circle should think about where his first touch is taking him.

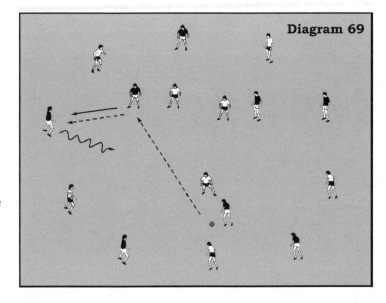

Diagram 69

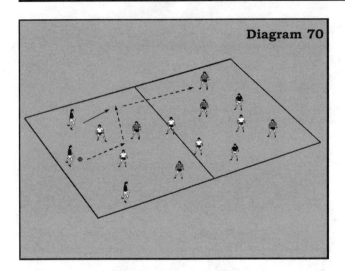

Diagram 70

5 v 5 v 5

Organize three teams of five, each team in a different colored jersey. Play on a rectangular field. The size will be determined by the age and ability level of the players. Two teams of five combine to play 10 v 5 keep-away from the other team of five. The team that is responsible for losing possession becomes the defending team.

Coaching Points

- Vary the length of the passes - short and long
- Play a few short passes to draw the defenders into that space then hit a long pass to the opposite side of the field
- Find space - don't get drawn in toward the ball
- Communicate - call for the pass if you are open

F.C. Petrolul Ploeisti - Youth Team

Submitted by Alexander Szasz, Director of Coaching for ESA of the USA. This session was conducted by Constantin Moldoveanu, Director of Youth Development at FC Petrolul Ploiesti of the Romanian First Division. The practice focuses on maintaining possession and applying quick pressure as a group in the defensive zone.

The following exercises are designed to give the defenders practice at bringing the ball out from the defensive zone. The same practice is also used to work on the forwards to give them practice at pressing the defenders, stealing possession and building a quick counter-attack. The defenders score one point for every goal. The attackers score one point for each attempt on goal or two points if they score.

Attack v Defense

Organize the defenders in groups of three and the attackers in groups of three. The attackers are positioned about 45 yards from goal. Place flags to mark two goals on the 45-yard line as shown in diagram 71. The goalkeeper starts the exercise by passing to a defender. As soon as the first pass is made, the three forwards cross the line and attempt to win possession from the defenders. The objective for the defenders is to score a goal by dribbling through one of the goals on the 45-yard line. The objective for the attackers is to pressure the defenders, steal the ball and mount a quick counter-attack with an attempt on goal.

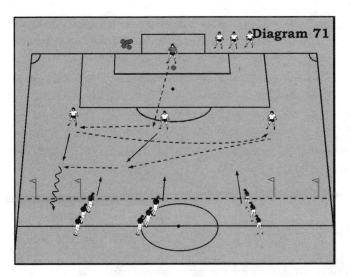

Diagram 71

Coaching Points

- Defending team has to make a minimum of four passes before they can score
- Quality passing by the defending team
- Defenders should use the full width of the field
- Attackers should make an attempt on goal as quickly as possible once they have won possession

Progression

Play 4 v 4 as shown in diagram 72.

Variations

There are many variations of this exercise that can be used depending on what area you want to focus on. For instance, if you are working on the attackers you could have the number of players in their favor by playing four attackers against three defenders. This would give them more opportunities to win possession and mount quick counter-attacks.

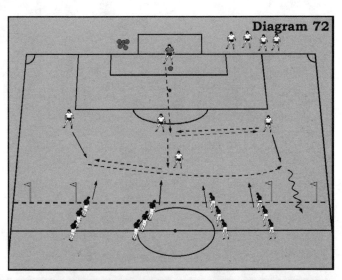

Diagram 72

F.C. Petrolul Ploeisti - Youth Team

3/4 Field Game

Mark a 3/4 size field with lines extending from the penalty area and the goals on the 18-yard line as shown in diagram 73. Play 3 v 3 plus goalkeepers in each half. The players must stay in their own half. The goalkeeper starts the game by passing to one of his defenders. The objective for the defenders is to complete a pre-determined number of passes in their own half. The forwards attempt to win possession and mount a quick counter-attack on goal. If the defenders achieve the pre-determined number of passes, they get two points. The attackers get one point for an attempt on goal and two points if they score. The defending team can pass the ball to their teammates in the other half if they have no passing options in their own half. The defenders on one half are teamed with the attackers in the other half and combine points against the other team.

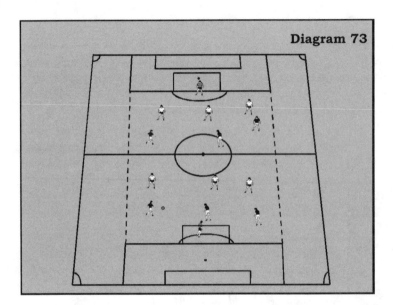

Diagram 73

Coaching Points

- All previous coaching points
- Forwards should defend as a team and not individuals
- If the forwards are unable to win possession, their next option is to force the defenders into passing to the opposite half before they reach their set number of passes

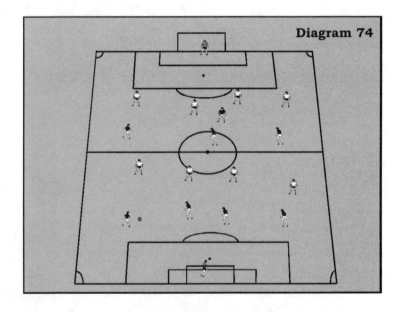

Diagram 74

Progression

Play 4 v 4 in each half on a full field as shown in diagram 74.

Variations

There are many variations that can be used depending on what area you want to focus on. For instance, if you are working on the attackers you could have the number of players in their favor by playing five attackers against four defenders. This would give them more opportunities to win possession and mount quick counter-attacks.

John Walker

This session conducted by John Walker, Nebraska University Women's Coach, was conducted at the WORLD CLASS COACHING International Coaching Seminar in Kansas City, February 9-11, 2001. The session was conducted indoors. The size of the area used for the sessions would be larger when practicing outdoors and would depend on the age and ability level of the players.

Exercise One

Organize two groups of eight players with one group per grid and two balls per group. The players move around their grid passing and receiving, playing two-touch. Various conditions are placed on the players:

- Must shout the name of the receiver before you pass them the ball
- Must shout the name of the passer before you receive the ball
- Must receive the ball sideways on, control and pass to another player with second touch
- As the ball is in flight, the receiving player must look around and decide who they will pass the ball to as quickly as possible
- Receiving player must let the ball run past them or across their body before passing with one touch
- Supporting players must provide an angle of support behind the receiver so that when the receiver lets the ball run past them they are in a position to receive the ball first time
- Players must locate the second ball so that both balls are not passed into the same player at the same time

The exercise then develops into a competition between the two groups. Players play two-touch with two balls as before. If either ball goes out of play, stops or hits the other ball then it is a point for the other team. Keep score, first team to five points wins.

The players are then told they can't talk, clap or make any sounds to get the attention of the passer. This forces the passer to lift their head up and look around. It forces the receiver to provide better angles of support and move into the visual path of the passer in order to receive the ball. The conditions make the game more demanding and competitive.

A third ball is introduced to each group and the players have unlimited touches. The players focus on where the other two balls are in the grid. Passers are asked to think of the other two balls as defenders and not to put players under pressure by playing balls into the same area but to try and keep the three balls away from each other. Players are then allowed to talk. The exercise finishes with players restricted to two-touch and scoring as before.

Coaching Comments

- Emphasize looking up, seeing the field, communication and movement on and off the ball throughout the session
- Ask players to play relaxed passes, not heavy ones
- Passes should be played comfortably into feet or space forcing players to concentrate on the weight of the pass
- The restriction on talking forces players to concentrate more on passing, control and support
- Point out how the level of passing improves when they can't talk as the players are forced to concentrate on technique

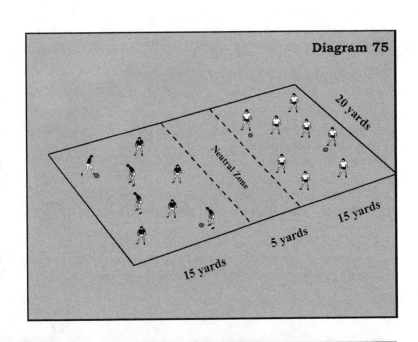

Diagram 75

Neutral Zone

20 yards

15 yards

5 yards

15 yards

John Walker

Exercise Two

Organize two grids with four quadrants (A, B, C and D) and a neutral area between the grids as shown in diagram 76. Two balls are placed in each quadrant with two groups of eight players. Players pass and move using two-touch in their starting quadrant, group 1 in A, group 2 in C. If they keep possession for 20 seconds without making a mistake (ball out of grid, balls hitting each other, etc.) all eight players move to the opposite quadrant (Group 1 to B, group 2 to D). They try to keep possession of the two balls there for 20 seconds and then they return to their original quadrant (Group 1 to A, group 2 to C). First team back to their starting quadrant wins a point. Keep score. First team to five points wins.

Note: Walker has his players at the University of Nebraska play this activity in a series of one-minute games.

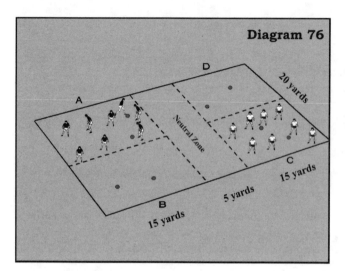

Diagram 76

Progressions

Same as before, but now the groups must rotate counter-clockwise. Group 1: A to B to C to D to A. Group 2: C to D to A to B to C. First team back to starting quadrant wins a point. Keep score. First team to five points wins.

If a group catches up to the opposite group, they "pin" them and receive a point. This forces players to pass and move quickly and travel between quadrants as fast as possible to try and catch the other group.

Exercise Three

Set up grids and groups the same as exercise two. Now two defenders start in the quadrant to make 6 v 2. Use one ball to pass and move and play two-touch keep-away. Each group must complete four consecutive passes then move to the next quadrant as before (A to B, C to D, etc). Defenders try to stop the passes. Defenders can play balls out of play or keep possession and the six players must then win the ball back and try to complete the four passes. The first team back to their starting quadrant wins a point. Keep score. First team to five points wins. If a group catches up with the opposite group they "pin" them and receive a point. Rotate defenders each game.

Coaching Comments
- Stress communication especially when looking to receive the ball
- Stress constant movement off the ball to make and receive passes and to keep the ball away from the defenders
- Conditions to suit your needs could be placed on each game such as, complete four passes, complete five passes, do a certain number of give-and-go's, overlaps or take-over's

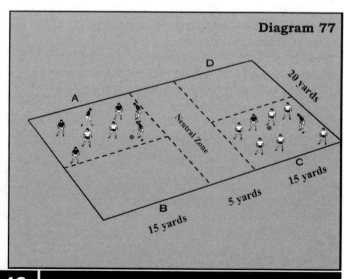

Diagram 77

John Walker

Exercise Four

In a 40 x 20-yard grid, organize four mini goals in each corner as shown in diagram 78 and eight players with two balls. Eight players can be resting or playing in a separate grid.

- Players play two-touch and pass and move around the grid
- Players try to pass through one of the goals to a teammate as often as possible
- Players can support behind or in front of each goal to receive a pass
- Players must interact with each other and try to move all over the grid, pass to every player, and receive from every player so that the activity does not become two groups within a group
- Count the number of goals scored in one minute - other team must try to beat the score
- Emphasis on type of pass used - push pass, driven, etc.
- If a player plays a ball through a goal, they must quickly support the receiver and get the ball back and try to switch the point of the attack
- Progress to one-touch
- Introduce one defender (8 v 1) who attempts to win the ball - the receiving player must find the defender and make runs into areas away from the defender
- Introduce a second defender (8 v 2)
- Introduce conditions such as two-touch, one-touch, combination play, third man running, etc.

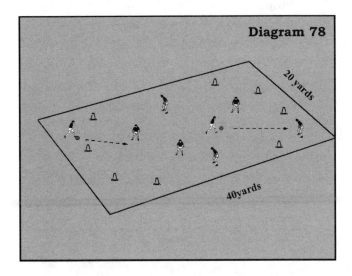

Diagram 78

Coaching Comments

- Activity forces players to be able to pass accurately
- When the activity goes to one touch, the talking stops as the technical demands get harder
- The one touch condition puts players under pressure forcing them to adapt to the pressure
- As players struggle with the conditions, balls go astray and talking stops

Exercise Five

Same area and goals as exercise four. Three players wear orange vests, three players wear blue vests and two players wear yellow vests. Players play two-touch as before and score a point by passing through a gate to a teammate. Three oranges or three blues team up with two yellows to make the game 5 v 3 or 3 v 3 + 2. If the defending team wins the ball, they become the attacking team.

Emphasis on short passes, pass to player in a central position, play a give-and-go with a player in a central position, play give and go between two defenders, pass to a player out wide, look for an overlapping runner, pass to furthest player away from you, make runs into space behind defenders. Keep score. First team to five points wins.

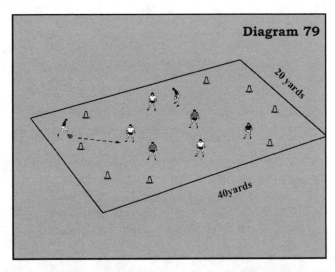

Diagram 79

Ajax U15 Youth Team

Contributed by subscriber, Terry Michler. Terry has been the coach at Christian Brothers College High School, St. Louis, MO for 30 years and has amassed a 602-159-74 record that includes 20 District Championships, nine State Final appearances and three State Championships. 230 of his former players have played college soccer and 32 have played professional soccer. Terry recently went on a 10-day trip to the Netherlands where he observed the training sessions of the Ajax professional and youth teams. This session, focusing on passing and possession, was conducted by the Ajax U15 team. Further sessions will appear in upcoming issues.

Passing

Using half a field, organize four players into set positions as shown in diagram 80. Player 1 starts with the ball and plays a drop-off pass to player 2. Player 2, who has made a flat checked run, plays the ball wide to player 3. Player 3 receives the ball side-ways on and plays the ball diagonally forward to player 4. Player 4 receives the ball with his back to goal and dribbles towards player 1 before passing the ball to him.

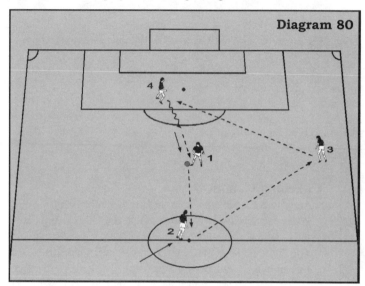

Diagram 80

Progressions
Increase the speed of movement and vary the range of passes.

Points
Players follow their pass and rotate positions accordingly.

Coaching Points
- Quality of the first touch
- Movement of players to receive the ball
- Range of passes used. Start with a side footed pass and progress to a lofted pass
- Encourage good communication

Variation

As shown in diagram 81, player 1 passes the ball to player 2 who receives it with a take-away. Following his spin, he plays a deep ball into player 4. Player 4, with his back to goal, moves the ball diagonally wide and passes to player 3. Player 3 then dribbles inside before releasing a square pass back to player 1.

Progressions
Increase the speed of movement and vary the range of passes.

Points
Players follow their pass and rotate positions accordingly.

Coaching Points
- Create angles and support the player with the ball.
- A great first touch sets up the ability to make a pass with your second touch

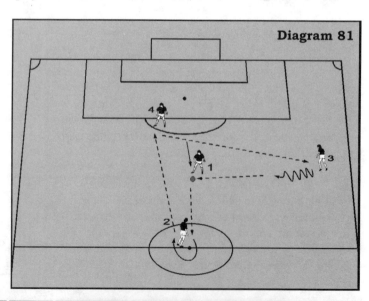

Diagram 81

Ajax U15 Youth Team

Possession Play

Set up a 10 x 10-yard area outside the penalty area placing 10 players into an 8 v 2 situation. Allow one-touch passes only and count the number of consecutive passes made. The defenders change place with the outside players either on a misplay, when 10 passes have been completed, or when the coach instructs.

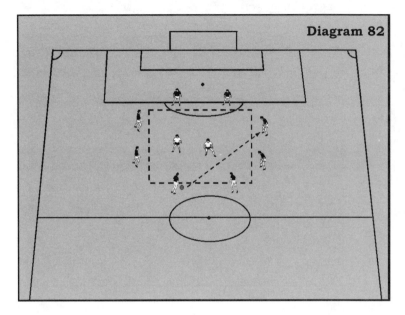

Diagram 82

Coaching Points
- Ensure that the angle of the pass is setting up the next player to play a quality pass
- Make sure that the weight of the pass is relevant to the length of the pass
- Focus on the quality of the first touch
- Encourage the awareness and availability of the outside players
- Play "on your toes"
- Encourage good communication from both the outside players and the defenders

Possession Play

Using the penalty area, organize seven players into a 4 v 3 situation and again count the consecutive passes made. Allow a two-touch condition and encourage the use of the deeper option. The defenders change place with the outside players either on a misplay, ten consecutive passes or at the coach's instruction.

Coaching Points
- Focus on the quality of the first touch to allow a better passing option with the second touch
- Encourage the awareness and availability of the outside players
- Play "on your toes"
- Look for the **deep** option
- Encourage good communication from both the outside players and the defenders

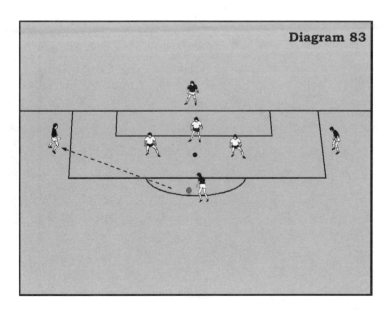

Diagram 83

Dallas Burn

Pre-season training with the Dallas Burn. As observed at Orlando, Florida - Pre-season 2001

Warm Up
Following a light jog and stretch, the squad broke down into groups of three, working on basic passing movements.

Organization
X1 passes to X2 and then runs at him and pressurizes the ball. X2 must take the ball to either side with a touch so as to avoid the pressure from X1. X2 then passes to X3 and pressurizes him. The drill continues as X3 passes to X1.

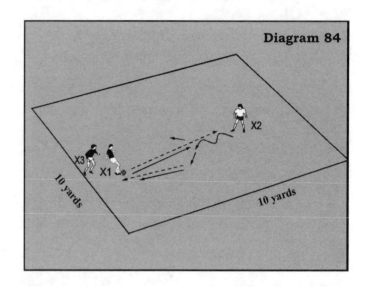

Diagram 84

Coaching Points
- Use of either the inside or outside of the feet to avoid pressure
- Use a variation of touches - one to control away from pressure and one to pass, sometimes two, three or more touches
- Add body fakes to beat the defender

Progression
The group progressed to a dribble-and-take drill. X1 dribbles towards X2. X2 runs to greet him in the middle. X1 leaves the ball for X2 to dribble onto X3. X2 leaves the ball for X3 who takes and dribbles towards X1 and so on.

Following the second drill, the groups stopped for water and to stretch a second time.

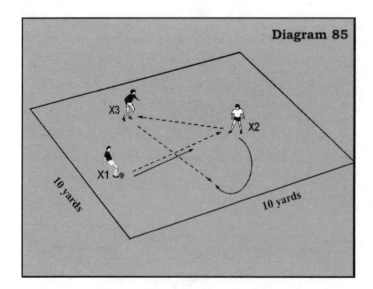

Diagram 85

Development
Still in groups of three using a wall pass, X1 passes to X2 and pressurizes. X2 passes to X3 and runs around and away from X1. X3 passes to X2 in his new position hence completing a wall pass. X2 then passes back to X3 and pressurizes. X3 completes a wall pass with X1 having run around X2. And so the drill continues.

Coaching Point
Communicating who passes to who next is the key to continuity.

Dallas Burn

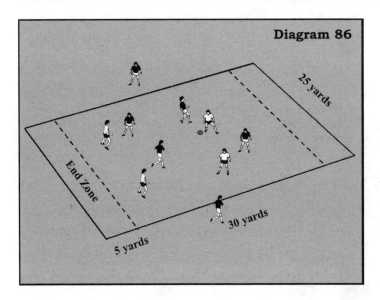

Diagram 86

Combination Plays

In diagram 86, the groups splits into 4 v 4 situations with two neutral players on the outside of the 30 x 25-yard playing area. The objective of the drill is for the team in possession to get the ball under control and into one of the end zones. If the team is successful, they keep the ball and attack the opposite end zone.

Conditions

- The outside players use one touch only
- Inside players are restricted to two touches
- To score, the players must receive the ball before entering the end zone

Progression One

Using the same area, the neutral players move to the end zones and act as target players. To score, the team in possession must receive the ball back from one of the neutral players. Following a goal, the team can then attack the opposite end zone.

Coaching Points

- Two-touch inside the area and one touch in the end zone
- Neutral players must move continuously to give an angle to receive the ball
- As soon as the target man is hit, the team must get players into position to receive the lay-off in order to score

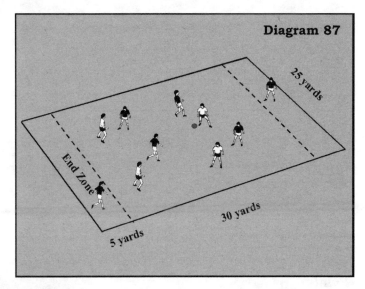

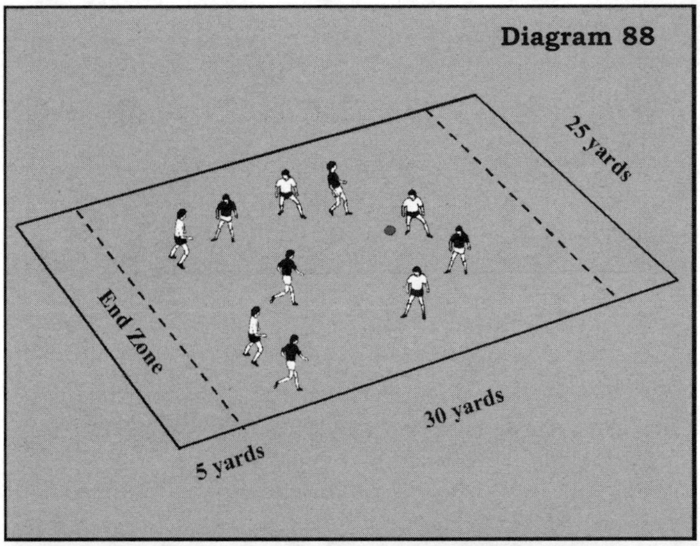

Diagram 87

Progression Two

Play 5 v 5 in the same area with teams having to get the ball under control in the end zone. Then once a goal is scored, instant transition to the opposite end zone is required.

Coaching Points

- Shape of the defense
- Defense to re-group following a goal
- The running and the movement off the ball
- The attackers must maintain their speed of play following a goal being scored
- Use and variation of the long and short options

Diagram 88

Dallas Burn

Progression Three

Following another water break, the practice is moved onto a 40 x 30-yard field. Using full-sized goals and goalkeepers, the group played 4 v 4 with neutral players on either side of the field.

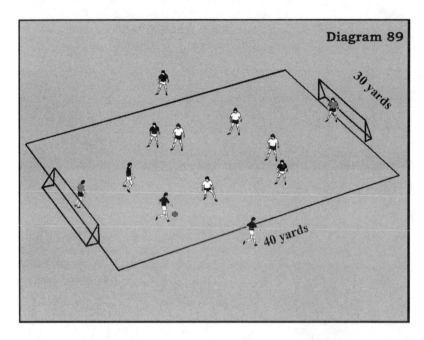

Diagram 89

Conditions

- The neutral players can only cross or pass the ball, not shoot
- Neutral players again have only one touch
- Unlimited touches allowed inside the field

Progression Four

The practice progresses to placing neutral players either side of the goal posts at both ends. The neutral players then act as target players who give lay-off's to the team in possession to shoot and score.

Points

Keep rotating the neutral players who only have one touch

Coaching Points

- Movement off the ball
- Work rate and continuity

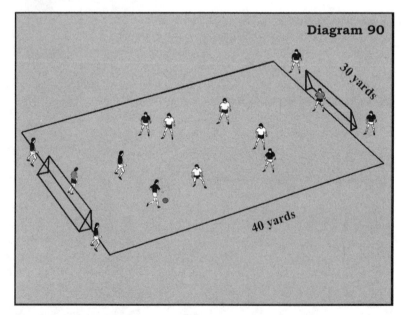

Diagram 90

General Points

For all the progressions, the coach wanted to work on combination plays, moving the ball quickly and highlighting the movement off the ball as the key to success. Water breaks were taken regularly throughout with the players work rate emphasized continuously. The session ended with a 5 v 5 game with unlimited touches followed by the coach giving the players time to work on individual aspects of their game such as, dribbling, control, shooting and passing.

Coaching Young Players

Contributed by Alex Mason, Director of Coaching for Millard Star/Arsenal Soccer Club of Omaha Nebraska. Alex has an English F.A. license, USSF "A" License and is a clinician for the National Youth Module. The following games are used to improve passing for players age six and older.

Organization: 10 v 10

Organize the players in a circle (size depending on age and ability) standing with their feet apart. Four players have a ball. On the whistle, the players with the balls dribble around the circle but must play the ball between each of the standing player's legs. The first player back to his starting position wins.

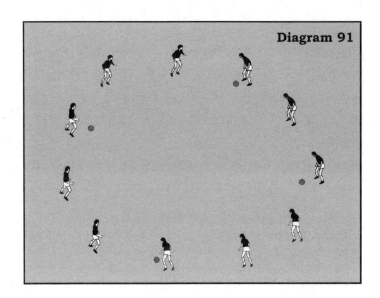

Diagram 91

Coaching Points

- Ball control
- Dribbling techniques
- Speed of play

Progression

The coach calls, "turn" and the players dribble in the opposite direction

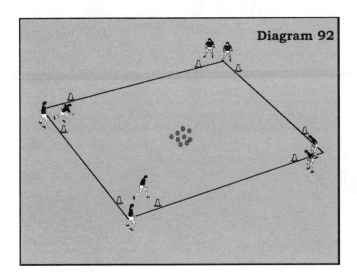

Diagram 92

The Fox - Passing

Organize two players in each goal. One player from each goal runs to collect the soccer balls and passes them back through the cones to his partner. Practice the following techniques: push pass, driven pass, juggle the ball back and chip to partner to catch with his hands.

Coaching Points

- Various passing techniques
- Receiving techniques
- Communication
- Speed of play

Coaching Young Players

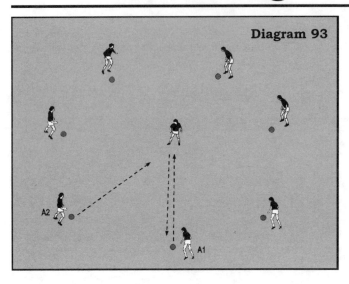

Diagram 93

A2

A1

Circle Passing

Organize the players, each with a ball, in a circle (size depends on age and ability of the players) and have one player in the center. Player A1 passes to the center player who controls and passes back to A1. A2 then passes to the center player and the game continues in clockwise direction. Play for a pre-determined amount of time or number of times around the circle for each center player, then change. Have two groups going at the same time so they can race each other.

Coaching Points
- Passing and receiving techniques
- Weight of pass
- Accuracy of pass

Passing and Receiving With Pressure

Organize four servers with balls outside a 10 x 10-yard grid. Two players, A and D, are in the center. Player A attempts to receive as many passes as possible from the servers. Player D attempts to steal the ball and not allow the passes. When player A receives a pass, he must return the pass to the server. Play for one minute and then change players.

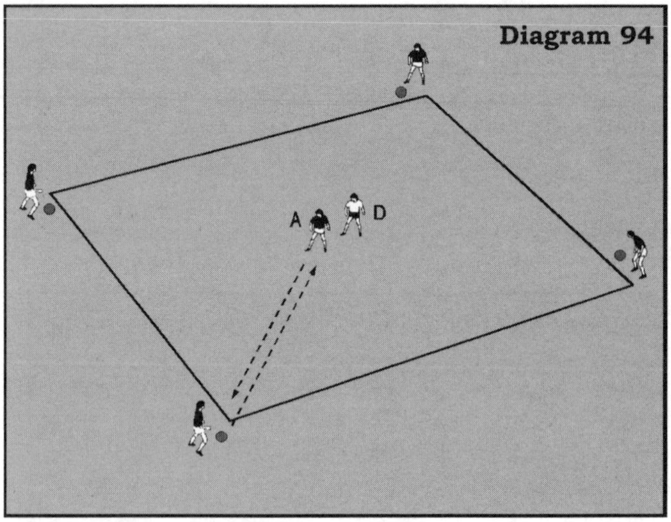

Diagram 94

A   D

Coaching Points
- Passing and receiving techniques under pressure
- Speed of play
- 1 v 1 tactics - create space
- Conditioning element

Progression
If player D steals the ball, he now becomes the receiver.

Diagram 95

D

A

Progression
The same game as in diagram 94. This time add more servers without balls. Player A receives from one server and returns the pass to a server without a ball.

These two games of receiving with pressure can be introduced once the players have developed good passing and receiving techniques unopposed.

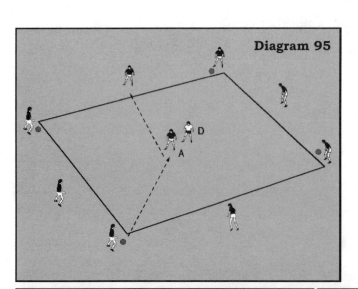

Barnsley F.C.

Contributed by long-time subscriber Gerry Canavan. Ten years ago at the age of 15 Gerry spent the summer training with Sheffield United, then in the English Premier League. At the time, Dave Bassett was the manager of Sheffield United. Over the last 10 years Gerry has been fortunate to visit Bassett as his coaching career has taken him to Nottingham Forest and now, Barnsley F.C. of the English First Division. In 2000, Gerry spent six weeks at Barnsley F.C. observing practices of all the teams and even training with the youth and reserve teams as well as helping to coach the younger Academy players. Gerry also traveled with the players and coaching staff as he observed the games of the first team, reserves and youth teams. Gerry is an active coach (USSF "A" License and NSCAA Advanced Diploma) in his home town of Chicago where he is Director of Coaching for the Wilmette Wings S.C.

Warm Up
This session was held on a Friday, a day before a league game. The players went through a standard jog and stretch routine for 20 minutes. The first team then spent 30 minutes practicing free kicks and corner kicks. The reserve team undertook drills focusing on passing, receiving and moving in tight spaces.

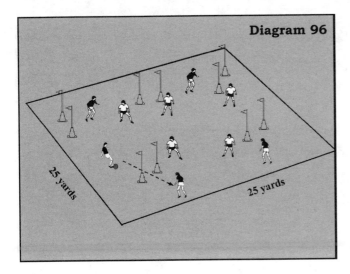

Diagram 96

25 yards

25 yards

Organization
In a 25 x 25-yard area, two teams of five play each other under various conditions. Five gates are set up within the area and the players score points in various ways. In diagram 96, players score points by passing through a gate to a teammate.

Conditions
You can not score back-to-back goals in the same gate.

Coaching Points
• Good first touch and quality passing
• Shift body shape in relation to the movement of the ball
• Do not force it through a gate, instead keep possession by changing the attack

Condition Two
In diagram 97, the players score goals by dribbling through a gate.

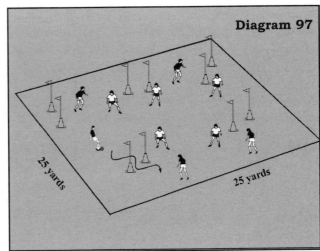

Diagram 97

25 yards

25 yards

Barnsley F.C.

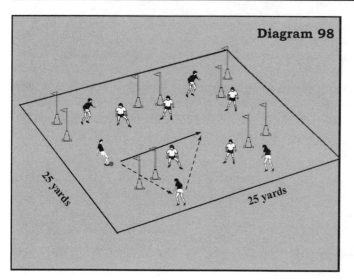

Diagram 98

Condition Three
In diagram 98, players score goals by playing a give-and-go through the gate.

Observations
The group played four 10-minute games with two minutes rest. The small area demanded a quality first touch, crisp passing, short explosive sprints, and quick decision making. The rule of not scoring back-to-back through a goal caused play to switch quickly and the small area forced each player play with one or two touches, so no other restrictions were required.

Scrimmage
The session ended with a scrimmage. Using an area from penalty area to penalty area, the team played an unconditioned game of 9 v 9 with goalkeepers.

Points
One-touch finishing was encouraged along with quality crossing and finishing, however, play was never stopped to emphasize anything specific.

Warm Down
The team jogged and stretched for 10 minutes.

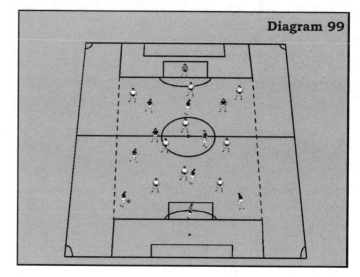

Diagram 99

Colorado Rapids

Pre-season training with the Colorado Rapids. As observed at Orlando, Florida - Pre-season 2001.

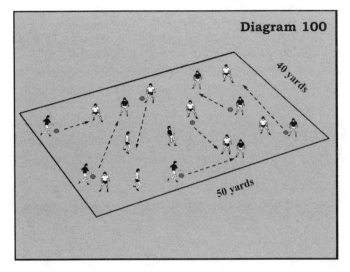

Diagram 100

40 yards

50 yards

Warm-Up
After 10 minutes of jogging and stretching, the 18 players worked in pairs undertaking various activities:
1. Jockeying - one player runs at his partner without the ball. His partner shuffles backwards mirroring his partners actions.
2. The players face each other and have to touch his partner's knees to win a point.
3. Players bunny hop over their partner and then move through their legs five times before switching.
4. Players start back-to-back with their arms interlocked, and on their coaches command, swing their partner either left or right.

The warm-up session ended with some running through ladders.

Organization
In a 50 x 40-yard area, the 18 players use seven balls to casually pass, dribble and move amongst themselves (see diagram 100).

Progression
In the same area as shown in diagram 101, the players organize themselves into three teams of six and play 6 v 6 with the remaining six players on the outside of the area playing for the team in possession. Ten complete passes count as a goal and the teams rotate every five minutes.

Conditions
Two touch inside the area and one touch outside.

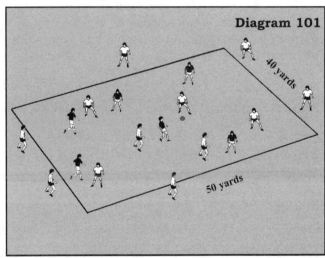

Diagram 101

40 yards

50 yards

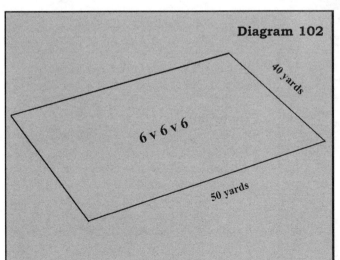

Diagram 102

40 yards

6 v 6 v 6

50 yards

Progression
Again using the same area, the teams play 6 v 6 v 6. All three teams play two teams versus one. The team that gives up possession automatically becomes the defending or 'odd' team.

Conditions
• Play two touch
• Continuous play when possession changes from team to team

Colorado Rapids

Progression
Using a full-sized field, the coach organized a possession/transitional game.

Organization
Two teams play 6 v 6 in one half of the field with the dark team attacking the goal. If they managed to score, then they attack the opposite goal against the third team of six. If that team then gets possession, they have to get the ball into the neutral zone (marked area) before they can attack the opposite goal and the other team.

Conditions
- Once a team has passed the ball out of the neutral zone, it cannot go back into the zone
- The ball must be moved continuously in the neutral zone until each team member enters the zone

Emphasis
The main emphasis is placed on transition. Teams are encouraged to play quickly and to have support on hand at all times. The coach emphasizes the necessity for good movement and for the defending team, once possession is gained, to move the ball quickly into the neutral zone in order to counter attack at speed.

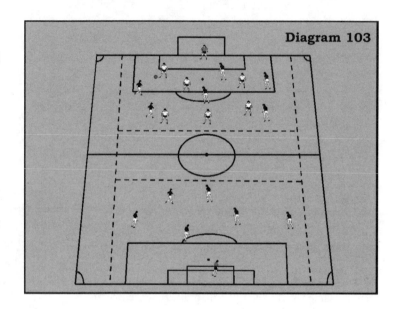
Diagram 103

Progression
The session ended with an 8 v 8 game with goalkeepers on a shortened field, but using the full width.

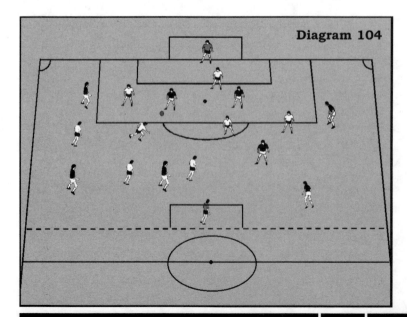
Diagram 104

Emphasis
The shortened field forces the players to get the ball out wide early and to counter attack from those positions.

Conditions
- No touch limitations
- No off sides
- No corners, goalkeepers take possession if the ball crosses the end line

Following the game, the team completed a warm down jog and stretch.

USYSA National Champions - U14G

Contributed by Mike Saif, editor and publisher of WORLD CLASS COACHING magazine. Mike participated in his first coaching course in his home country of England 20 years ago when he was just 19 years old. After arriving in the U.S. in 1991 Mike attended and passed the USSF "B" Licence in 1993 and the USSF "A" Licence in 1994.

Mike formed the 87 Dynamos Girls Team at the U10 age group although he had coached a number of the players in various other teams and clinics since they were 7 and 8 years old. Over the years the Dynamos have won a National Indoor Championship, three consecutive State Championships and a Region Two Championship before winning the 2001 USYSA/Snickers U14G National Championship. In this article, Mike explains what kind of schedule the team followed during their National Championship season and shares a typical training session.

After losing in the final of the Region Two tournament last year, I evaluated our strengths and weaknesses. I talked to a number of coaches of teams that had won their Regional or National tournaments to find out what kind of practice and game schedule they did with their teams.

Our practice schedule for the previous year was twice a week in the fall and spring and once a week indoors during the winter months (Nov - Feb). We did some conditioning but not much. For this year, we increased our practice schedule to three times a week for the fall and spring and still once a week during the indoor season. However, we did conditioning at most practices and the girls attended a voluntary strength, speed and agility (plyometric) workout twice a week at a health club during the indoor season.

Our conditioning workouts consisted of 800 - 1,500 yards of sprints with a maximum distance of 300 yards down to 10 yard shuttles. These lasted about 20 minutes and were done during most training sessions.

Our game schedule didn't really change that much. We played 25 games in the fall including three tournaments. The spring season consisted of 24 games prior to playing in the Region Two tournament in late June. During the winter months we played about 10 - 12 indoor games.

After winning the Kansas State Cup, we practiced Monday through Thursday in the mornings for two weeks prior to Regionals. We also scheduled 7 or 8 scrimmage games during the evenings and at the weekend. After the Regional tournament we took 10 days off and repeated the same two week practice schedule prior to the National tournament.

As the editor and publisher of WORLD CLASS COACHING magazine I have been fortunate to visit and observe some of the best youth coaches in the world. Much of my training sessions are based on what I have observed and learned from these coaches. Much of what we do is based around a possession game, therefore we work constantly on passing and receiving. This year I introduced more tactical awareness such as how to break down other teams, playing against the offside trap, switching the point of attack, etc.

We play a very attacking 4-4-2 or 2-4-4 formation (this year we scored 198 goals and conceded only 18 from 58 games). Our two wide midfielders play as attacking wingers when we have possession and our two fullbacks push up as midfielders. There is an element of risk involved but we feel we are capable of scoring more goals than we concede playing this way. Our two center defenders are also extremely quick, strong and good 1 v 1 defenders which enables us to take those risks. Plus it is much more fun for the players to play an attacking style.

On reflection, the factors that were important in us winning the National Championship were less to do with technique and tactics and more to do with the mental side of the game:

Conditioning - We felt that we were at least as fit if not fitter than every team we faced. The plyometric workouts also made a difference and helped reduce injuries.

Practice Schedule - What amounted to practice in the morning and a scrimmage in the afternoon for two weeks prior to Regionals and Nationals was critical. We improved so much during that time, probably as much as we had improved during the entire spring season.

Commitment and Dedication - For the entire year, no player missed a game other than for an injury. We also had an excellent attendance for practices with 12 of 15 girls missing only one or no practices for the entire spring/ summer season.

Team Goal - After losing in the final last year, the players set their goal to win Regionals this year and constantly talked about it during the season. This is what they used to push themselves during conditioning workouts.

Team Chemistry - Without doubt, team chemistry was critical. Without it we would have struggled to overcome the hurdles and setbacks we faced during the season. The girls love soccer, love playing with each other and have a great time at practice, games and out-of-town tournaments.

A typical training session of the 2001 USYSA U14G National Champions, KC Dynamos contributed by head coach, Mike Saif.

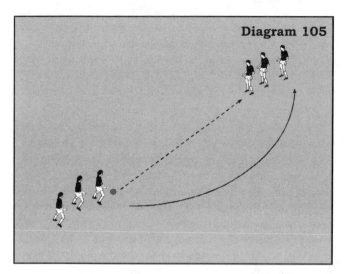

Diagram 105

Warm-Up

The players arrive about 15 minutes before the scheduled practice time and go through a jog and stretch routine. The warm-up with the ball starts with players in groups of five or six. Each group forms two lines 15 yards apart as shown in diagram 105. The front player in line passes the ball to the opposite line and follows her pass to join the back of that line. The drill continues with the ball being passed between the two lines of players. Play for 5 - 10 minutes with breaks for stretches.

Variations

Throughout the season we do many variations of this drill such as shortening or lengthening the distance between the two lines, limiting the number of touches or playing a give-and-go as shown in diagram 106.

Coaching Points

- A good first touch to keep the ball on the ground and in front to allow for a quick pass to the opposite line
- Firm accurate passes
- Play as quickly as possible
- Pass and receive using different surfaces of the foot

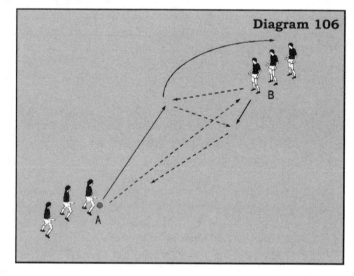

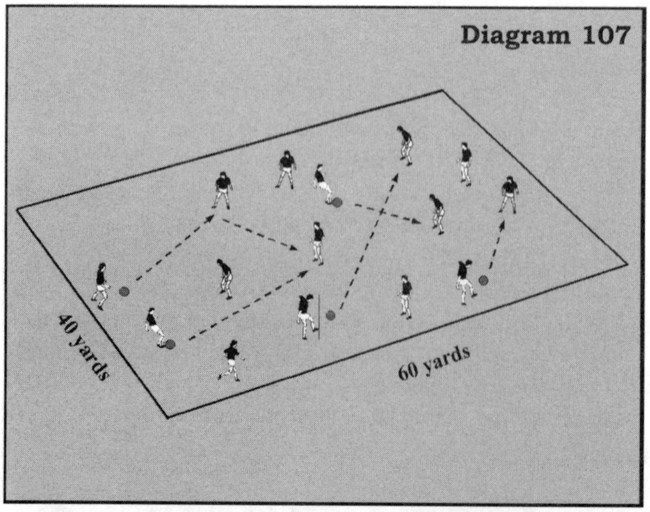

Diagram 106

Passing and Receiving

Using 5 or 6 balls, all 16 players pass and move around inside a 60 x 40-yard area. The objective of the game is to keep moving and have the players constantly showing and asking for players to pass to them. Occasionally, we might add 2 or 3 defenders to ensure the players are also focusing on what is happening around them as they receive the ball.

Coaching Points

- Show and ask for passes
- Move into the spaces with and without the ball
- When in possession, keep your head up to see your options
- Play at game speed

Diagram 107

40 yards

60 yards

One-Touch Passing

I got this game from observing Ray Hudson coaching the Miami Fusion at pre-season training earlier this year. Split the players into two teams. With 16 players I use a 60 x 40-yard area. If there is an odd number, use a "neutral" player who plays for the team in possession. The teams play keep-away but only the one-touch passes are counted. The first team to 20 passes is the winning team. Play two or three games. This game can be used for working on passing and receiving or on closing down defensively.

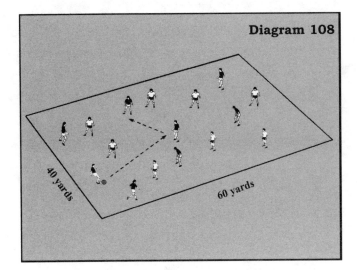

Diagram 108

40 yards

60 yards

Coaching Points

• Awareness - know where you are going to pass the ball before you receive it
• Only use a one-touch pass if it's on - if not use two or more touches to ensure you keep possession
• Quality passes and receiving touches
• Work hard to get open to receive a pass - it makes it easier for the person in possession
• Once you lose possession try to get it back as soon as possible
• Play at game speed

Progression

Place one player from each team on the end-line as shown in diagram 109. Now the teams must keep possession with a directional objective of passing the ball to their target player on the end-line.

Coaching Points

• Possession with a purpose - play forward if possible
• Use all previous coaching points
• Play at game speed

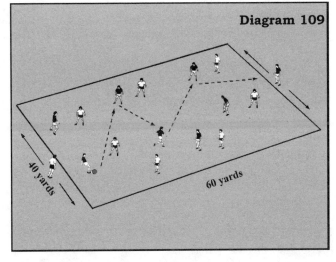

Diagram 109

40 yards

60 yards

Conditioning

The conditioning part of practice is a series of sprints with adequate rest in between each set of sprints to allow the heart rate to get back to about 75% normal rate. The maximum sprint we do is about 300 yards and the shortest sprint we do is 10 yards. At the early part of the season we tend to do more of the longer sprints and toward the end of the season we will do more of the shorter sprints. I split the team into three groups with each group containing players with similar speed and endurance. This adds an element of competition as the players are all expected to finish each sprint in close proximity of each other. Having three groups allows for one sprint followed by three parts rest with a break after each set of sprints to allow 75% recovery. A typical session is as follows:

2 x 300-yard sprints
3 x 150-yard sprints
5 x 50-yard sprints

Chelsea F.C. Youth Academy

This training session was designed for the Prince William Sparklers U17 Girls, by Chelsea F.C. Youth Academy. The Prince William Sparklers were the 2000 U16 Region One Champions and spent 10 days in England sponsored by the Inter-national Academy. The article is submitted by Sparklers coach Ken Krieger, USSF "A" License, VYSA and Region One ODP staff coach.

Youth Development Officer, Paul Murphy led the first session which was a very light session in preparation for an afternoon game against the Fulham Lionesses, England's first full-time professional women's team.

Warm Up
Using a 20 x 20-yard grid, the girls first divided into pairs, each pair with a ball. The girls juggled in a variety of ways to warm up.

Progression
The session then progresses into simple commands with the coach shouting "1" for the girls to exchange juggles with one touch. Then "2", "3", "4", and up to ten. Further progressions include everyone having a ball. As the players juggle, the coach shouts "change' and the girls then exchange balls from one another without losing control of their juggling. To finish, ball tag was played. Everyone has a ball and on the coach's command "GO", the girls are instructed to chase and "tag" only their partner without losing control of their ball.

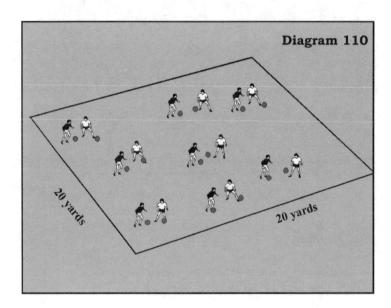

Diagram 110

20 yards
20 yards

Coaching Point
Keep the ball within the framework of your body.

Circle Drill
Eight players are inside a circle 20 yards in diameter with eight players, each with a ball, around the circumference. Players in the middle initially move away from a teammate then check to a ball quickly using a variety of skills. Players work time should be approximately one to two minutes each.

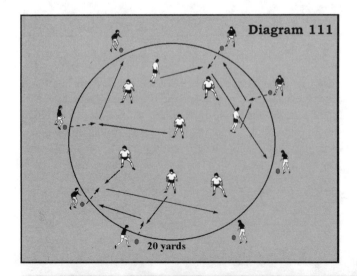

Diagram 111

20 yards

Variations
- Players receive the ball and tap it ten times between the inside of their feet before returning it to a teammate.
- Step on the ball five times, alternating touches quickly.
- Play a one-touch pass back to a teammate.
- Side foot volleys, receive ball on chest or thigh, take a bounce away quickly from the floor, pass the ball to a different teammate.
- Turns; players have the opportunity to be creative, turn out, spin out etc.
- Emphasis on staying low in the turn and accelerating away quickly.

Cool Down
Jogging in two's, with a variety of stretches.

Chelsea F.C. Youth Academy

This training session is a regeneration session and was done the day after a game.

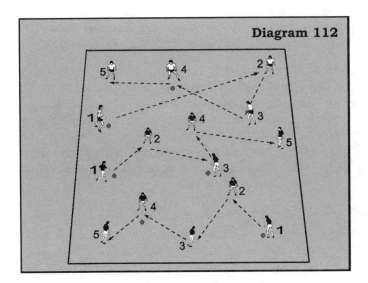

Diagram 112

Warm Up
Players line up in two's and jog around the field doing simple rhythm exercises with the coach. Players start with a two-step sequence to the right and then the left (side to side). This is followed by a series of quick sprints and then a turn and a jog to the end of the line followed by stretches.

Game
In a 50 x 30-yard area, the players divide into three teams of five and number one through five. Using no more than three touches, the players pass in sequence on the move with two balls for each group. Emphasis is placed on vision, good control, first touch and accuracy in passing on the move.

Progression
Players then pair off with one player in yellow and the other in blue. Using two balls in the same area, the blue team plays "keep ball" possession while the yellow team defends.

Conditions
If a yellow wins the ball, they dribble outside the grid and leave the ball for blue to pick back up and play again. After several sequences, the coach then adds a third ball, one in each half and one in the middle .

Coaching Point
Emphasis on communication and information "on the ball".

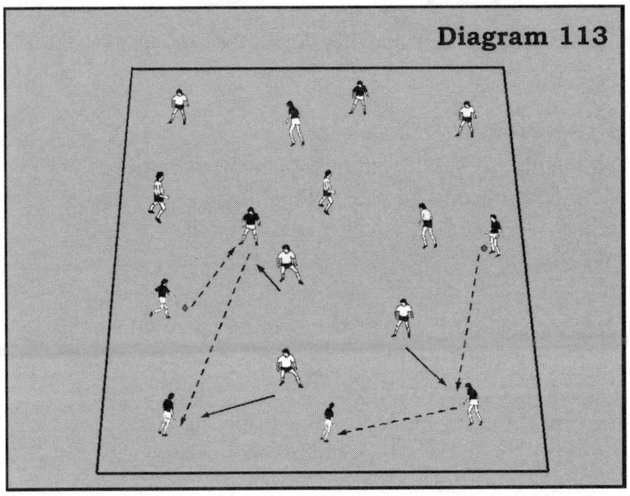

Diagram 113

8 v 8 + 1
Using half a field with two small goals at each end, two teams of eight play with a neutral player that plays for the team in possession.

Coaching Points
• Emphasize stretching the team wide and long
• Work to get defenders moving backwards, stretching the game and not condensing the space for attacking players to play in.

Warm Down
Using hurdles, ladders and cones, the players ran over the hurdles, zig zagged around cones and finished with some quick steps over the poles.

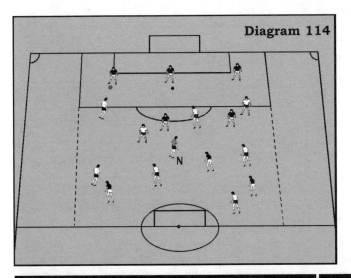

Diagram 114

Juventus F.C.

This article is contributed by subscriber Dave Brown and is part of the Juventus Journal, the new "Free Bonus" we are offering to new and existing subscribers. Brown took part in an overseas coaching tour to the Juventus pre-season training village Sponsored by GoPlay Sports Tours. Visit their web site at www.goplaytours.com or see their ad inside the back page for more details of their overseas coaching tours. This is a session from the Juventus team that included all their well known players such as Conte, Davids, Del Pierro, Montero, Nedved, Thuram, Trezeguet and Zambrotta.

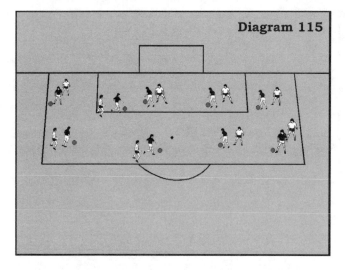

Diagram 115

Technical Work In Pairs

While three goalkeepers work at the opposite end of the field with their coach, 18 field players work in pairs in the penalty area. They do each of the following exercises for two minutes each, changing roles on the coaches signal every minute and doing light stretching in the 30-second rest period between each drill.

- One player dribbles the ball, feinting and changing direction in a small area shadowed by his partner who doesn't make a tackle, but who stays close to his opponent
- One player now shields the ball from his partner, staying in a small area, shifting the ball from one foot to another depending on the defender's position

Progression

Following a break for stretching, the players move freely passing and moving without direction. They no longer work just with their partners and there is still only one ball for each two players.

- Players with the ball dribble while those without call for the ball to receive short passes. Upon receiving the ball, they move quickly away to a new position
- After receiving the ball from a dribbling player, they return it with one touch and immediately spin away calling for the next ball

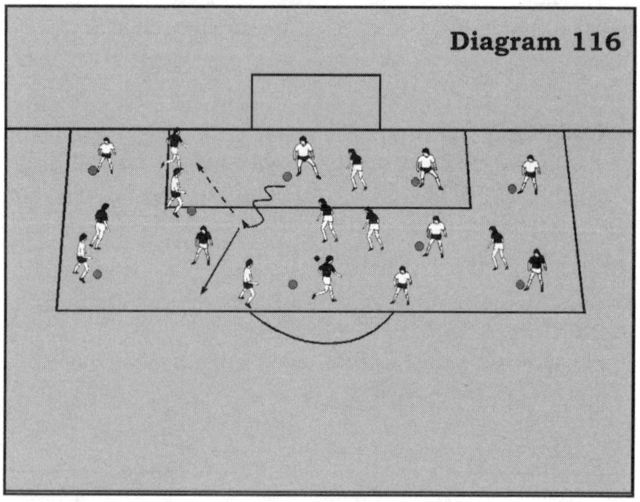

Diagram 116

Progressions

Similar, but now the dribbling player approaches a player slowly and then plays a quick wall pass and accelerates onto the return pass.

Now have one ball between three players. The dribbling player, working with a teammate, "attacks" a defender and combines with his teammate for a wall pass around him. After the move is complete, the defender then takes the ball and initiates his own wall pass.

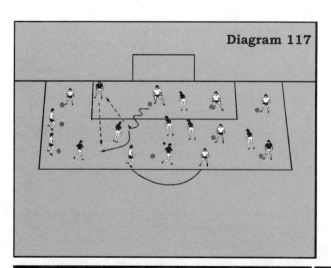

Diagram 117

Juventus F.C.

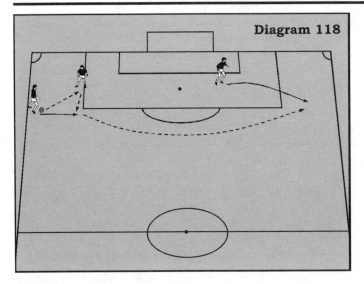

Diagram 118

Progression - Third Man Runs

The size of the work area is expanded to use the full width of the pitch. This last exercise in the series is similar to the previous, except that the final ball is now played close to 40 or 50 yards in length. The goal is to hit a running teammate with a flighted ball after two players combine with two short passes. (The distances can be shortened depending on the standard of the players involved.)

Possession Exercises 6 v 6 + 6

Play 6 v 6 keep-away in the marked area with the six remaining "neutral" players on the outside of the field supporting the team in possession. The aim of the game is for the six players to maintain possession before playing to one of the neutral players who then plays a one-touch pass to the perimeter player opposite. The receiving players's successfully controlled long pass equals one point. The neutral team alternates with one of the inside teams on a time basis.

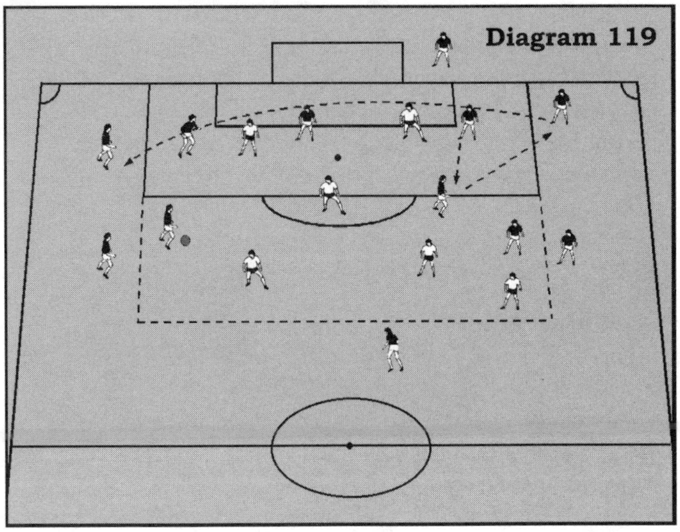

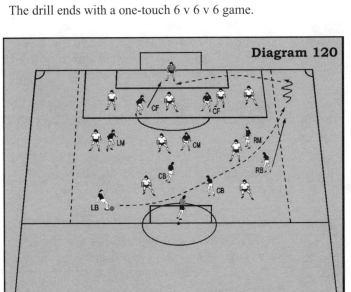

Diagram 119

Coaching Point

The level of passing technique, control, speed of defending and concentration required is extremely high for this drill to succeed.

The drill ends with a one-touch 6 v 6 v 6 game.

Diagram 120

Crossing Game

Play 10 v 10 in one half of the field, with neutral channels on each flank. Any one player at a time can enter the channel to produce a cross (but can not be challenged by a defender). Both teams line up in a 4-3-2 formation. The emphasis of the drill is quality long flighted balls into the attacking zones followed by quality crosses and attacking runs.

The session ends with a no-restrictions scrimmage followed by three cool down laps of the field and some 'indoor' stretching.

David Williams

David Williams conducted a session at the WORLD CLASS COACHING International Coaching Seminar, Connecticut, June 2000, that included various exercises focusing on technique development for youth players. All the exercises can be used as warm-ups for just about any practice or they could be included as part of a typical training session to improve techniques.

Passing and Receiving Techniques

Organize two groups of three players in a 40 x 20-yard area with one ball per group. The players pass and move doing the following techniques. Each technique was done for two minutes. The size of the area can be altered depending on the number of players.

Techniques

- Receive with the inside of the foot and immediately move away pushing the ball with the outside of the same foot.
- Receive using the same technique as above but this time use softer passes and sprint away for 5-10 yards after receiving the ball.
- Control with an open body position and move away.
- Control with the outside of the foot and move away.
- Firm passes, short and long, as required in a game situation - receive using a variety of the previous techniques.

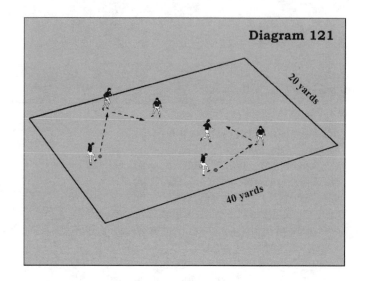

Diagram 121

Coaching Points

- The players without the ball make runs to create space before receiving the ball - the player with the ball must look for these runs
- Vary the runs - come short and spin to receive a long pass, go long and come short to receive a short pass, etc.
- The passer and receiver must have a good understanding and good communication - the receiver goes to the ball when the passer looks up
- The third player must create an angle and space to receive a one-touch pass from the receiving player

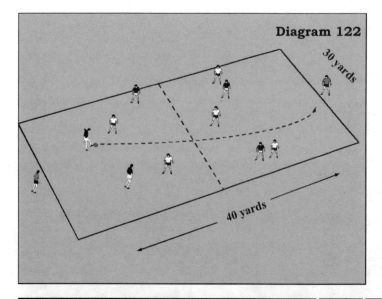

Diagram 122

Small-Sided Game

In a 40 x 30-yard area, play 5 v 5 with a target man on each end line. Score by passing from your own half to a target player on the end-line.

Coaching Points

- Only make the pass if it's on, do not force the long pass
- Keep possession until the pass is on
- Use the same turns and receiving techniques practiced in the previous drills.

Progression

Play with man-for-man markers. The aim is to lose your marker. Give one point if the players can perform a receiving technique practiced in the earlier exercises.

David Williams

In this session, David Williams showed a number of circle practices designed to develop quick play. There are literally hundreds of different variations of these circle practices and others that can be used as part of your training sessions.

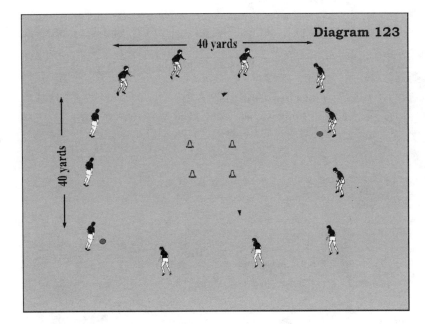

Diagram 123

Warm-Up
Organize the players in a 40-yard circle with four cones placed in the center as shown in diagram 123. Start with two balls. Dribble into the center square, dribble out and pass to another player, then take his place on the circle perimeter.

Add the following conditions:
- Left/right foot only
- Perform a turn in the center
- Change of pace, go in slow, come out fast.
- Change direction

Coaching Points
- Don't let gaps appear on the circle perimeter
- Communicate, and move around the edge to fill any spaces
- Start with two balls - add or take away balls as necessary

Progression
Once the player has been through the center square, instead of passing the ball to another player, the receiving player 'takes' the ball in a take-over move.

Give-and-Go
In this example, player A dribbles the ball into the center of the circle and passes to player B. Player B passes back with one touch to player A who then passes one touch to player C. Player C continues the drill by dribbling into the center of the circle. Again, start with two balls and adjust accordingly. This exercise helps build quick play around the goalbox.

Coaching Points
- One-touch passes if possible
- Always be ready 'off' the ball
- Fill the gaps around the circle as the players move
- Be aware of where the other balls are and don't dribble to that area
- Try to increase the speed of drill
- The 'set up' pass must be of good quality to allow the next player to pass with one touch

This exercise helps the following:
- **Technical** - pace and angle of pass
- **Fitness** - sprinting, running
- **Mental** - always thinking

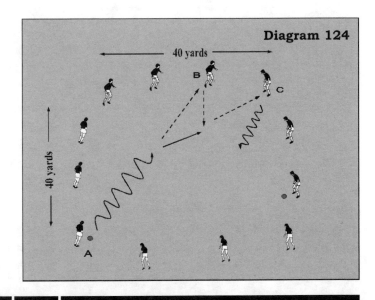

Diagram 124

David Williams

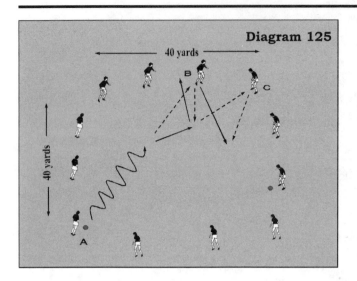

Diagram 125

40 yards

40 yards

B

C

A

Third Player Running

The same as the previous exercise, except this time after player B has made the return pass to player A, he moves into the center to receive the pass from player C. Player A moves into the spot vacated by player B.

Coaching Points

• Timing is vital - don't make your runs too early
• The ball must keep moving
• The third player must be aware of where he will receive the pass

Center Player

Start with a player who stays permanently in the center of the circle. Player A starts by passing to the center player, D. Player D plays a give-and-go with player A who then passes across the circle to player B. Player B continues the drill by passing to player D.

Coaching Point

• The player in the center 'runs' the drill, communication, speed, etc.

Progression

Add a second player in the center.

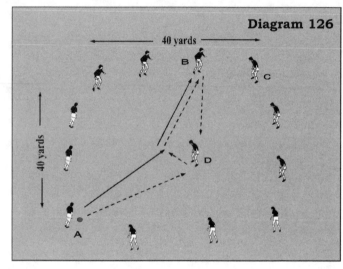

Diagram 126

40 yards

40 yards

B

C

D

A

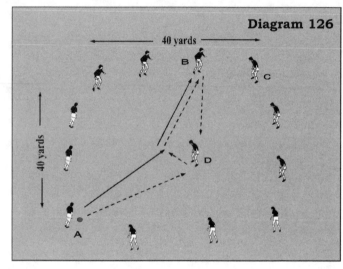

Diagram 127

40 yards

40 yards

D

C

B

A

Two Center Players

Start with two players in the center. Player A passes a firm pass to player B. Player B lays a pass into the path of player C. Player C passes across the circle to player D. Each player follows his pass.

Coaching Points

• Players on the outside must always be ready
• The central player 'without' the ball makes the decision for his team mate as to where to pass the ball

David Williams

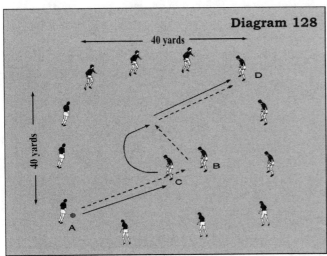

Diagram 128

Two Center Players

In this example, the players perform an "over". Player A passes to player C who allows it to run through his legs or by the side of him to player B. Player B lays the ball off into space for player C who has spun round into the space. Player C passes across the circle to player D.

Coaching Points

- Player B must be the one to shout "over" - this communicates to player C to let the ball run by him
- Player C must spin quickly to receive the ball

Small-Sided Game

End practice with an 8 v 8 game and look to incorporate all the moves learned during the circle practices.

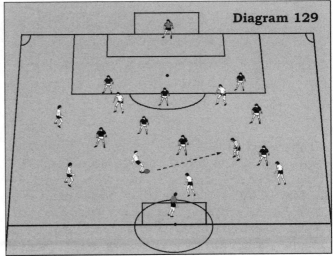

Diagram 129

Sammy Lee

Sammy Lee, Liverpool F.C. Assistant Manager, shared some exercises that are designed to improve the quality of passing, and the movement off the ball to find space to receive passes. The session starts with some warm-up drills progressing to unopposed pattern play and ends with a small-sided game.

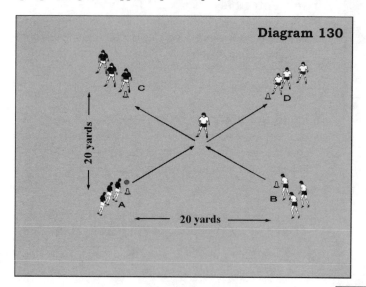

Warm-Up

Organize the players in a 20 x 20-yard area as shown in diagram 130, with a player in the center and players lined up at each cone. Only one ball is used. Player A carries the ball in his hands and runs toward the center player, passing him the ball and then joining the back of the opposite line. Player B starts his run a little after player A started his run, therefore he arrives in the center just after the center player has received the ball. The center player passes the ball to player B who carries it and passes it to the first player in the opposite line, player C. Player C continues the drill by carrying the ball to the center and passing it to the center player who then passes to incoming player D.

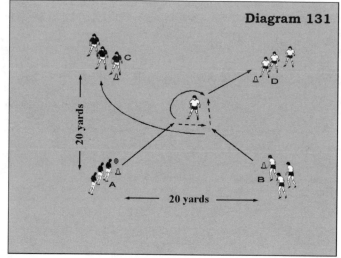

Progression

In this progression the timing of the runs is even more critical. The center player doesn't touch the ball. Player A carries the ball to the center. At the same time player B starts his run. Player A passes to player B then runs around the center player to receive the pass back from player B. Both players run to the opposite lines. Player A passes the ball to player D and the drill continues.

Pass and Follow

In the same 20 x 20-yard area, the players pass and follow their pass. The sequence is straight, diagonal, straight, etc. Start with two-touch and progress to one-touch.

Coaching Points

- Quality of the pass and receiving touch
- Use both feet
- Don't run across the area of the next pass
- Don't start running until you receive the ball

Sammy Lee

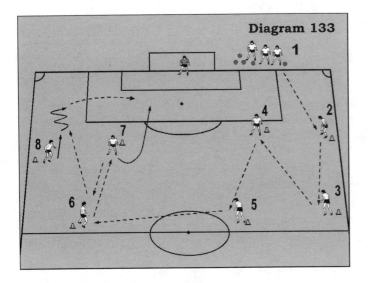

Diagram 133

Passing Combinations

This exercise emphasizes passing, movement and player rotation. Organize the players on a half-field as shown in diagram 133. Player 1 starts by passing to player 2, player 2 to player 3 and so on. Player 7 turns and runs into the penalty area to receive the cross from player 8. When the ball reaches player 6 the next ball can be passed in. Each player follows his pass. Many different combinations can be practiced using this exercise.

Coaching Points
- Two-touch
- Play as quickly as possible but still maintain control

Throw/Volley/Catch

Set up a 15 x 10-yard field with full-size goals and play 6 v 6 throw/volley/catch with no goalkeepers. Any player can attempt to stop a goal but cannot use his hands. Encourage the players to use their support players and think about creating angles and moving to receive the ball as they did in the earlier drills.

Coaching Points
- All previous coaching points
- Don't throw long balls - build the play with passing and moving

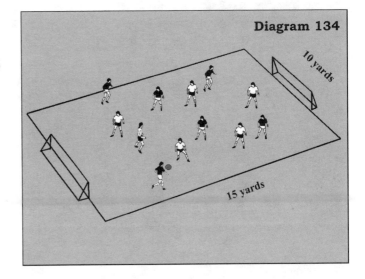

Diagram 134

10 yards

15 yards

OTHER BOOKS IN THIS SERIES

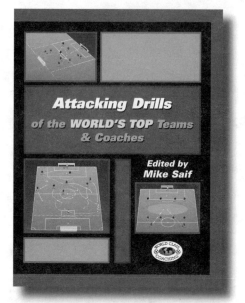

Attacking Drills of the World's Top Teams and Coaches includes training sessions and drills from **Manchester United, U.S. Women's World Cup Team, Venice of Serie "A", Liverpool F.C., Bodens BK of Sweden, Brazilian Youth Teams** plus many of the MLS Teams and other top teams and coaches from around the world.

Over 30 training sessions are included, each with detailed explanations accompanied with easy-to-read diagrams.

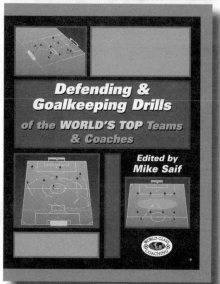

Defending and Goalkeeping Drills of the World's Top Teams and Coaches includes training sessions and drills from **Sao Paulo of Brazil, Italy U15 National Team, Tony DiCicco, Liverpool F.C., Lira Lulea BK of Sweden, Leeds United** plus **New England Revolution of the MLS** and other top teams and coaches from around the world.

Over 20 training sessions are included, each with detailed explanations accompanied with easy-to-read diagrams.

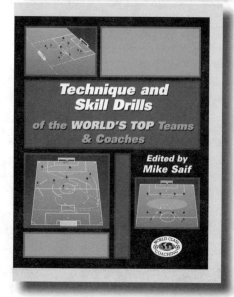

Technique and Skill Drills of the World's Top Teams and Coaches includes training sessions and drills from **PSV Eindhoven, U.S. Women's World Cup Team, Ajax F.C., Liverpool F.C., Leeds United, FK Teplice** plus many of the MLS Teams and other top teams and coaches from around the world.

Twenty-nine training sessions are included, each with detailed explanations accompanied with easy-to-read diagrams.

New Videotapes

Featuring Coaches of
Manchester United - Liverpool F.C. - Leeds United

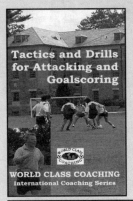

Tactics and Drills for Attacking and Goalscoring

#2001 Tactics and Drills for Attacking and Goalscoring - $34.95

Counter Attacking With Pace - Sammy Lee: A progression of quick passing and moving exercises with the ultimate objective of implementing them in an 11 v 11 game.

Improve Your Shooting and Finishing - Mick Hennigan: A session with an overall theme of "quality" finishing with an emphasis of shots hitting the target.

Build-Up Play For Crosses - Sammy Lee: Starts with a circle warm-up, progresses to a small-sided passing game and ends with a half-field game designed to get the ball wide for a cross.

Attacking In Waves - Sammy Lee: Some quick-fire shooting and finishing exercises, ending with a half-field game that includes overlapping defenders pushing forward and overloading the attack.

#2002 Tactics and Drills for Zonal Defending - $34.95

Defending With a Back Four - David Williams: This session starts with some individual defending and progresses to various exercises with two defenders and then four defenders. The session ends with four defenders working on a full field.

Zonal Defending - Mick Hennigan: A session designed to get the entire team familiar with their roles when the opposing team has possession. Based on a 4-4-2, the session could easily be adapted to a 3-5-2 or any other formation. Hennigan introduces "key words", and the actions that go with them that will enable each player to be comfortable and confident with his role and that of his teammates.

Improving Confidence For Heading - Mick Hennigan: A lively session that starts with heading warm-ups and progresses to game-like exercises that includes heading for goal as well as defensive heading.

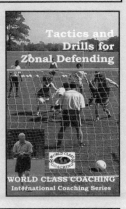

Tactics and Drills for Zonal Defending

Tactics and Drills for Passing and Possession

#2003 Tactics and Drills for Passing and Possession - $34.95

Developing Techniques For Youth Players - David Williams: This session includes various passing and receiving exercises and progresses to a small-sided game. The session also focuses on making the correct runs and angles to create space to receive passes.

Developing Quick Play Using Circle Practices - David Williams: This session was one of the highlights of the entire seminar and features a number of circle practices designed to develop quick play. Many variations are shown with unlimited variations possible with a little imagination.

Passing Progressions - Sammy Lee: This session is designed to improve the quality and speed of passing, and movement off the ball to create space to receive passes.

Buy All Three Tapes For Only $89.95

To Order call: 1-888-342-6224

Visit *worldclasscoaching.com* to order online

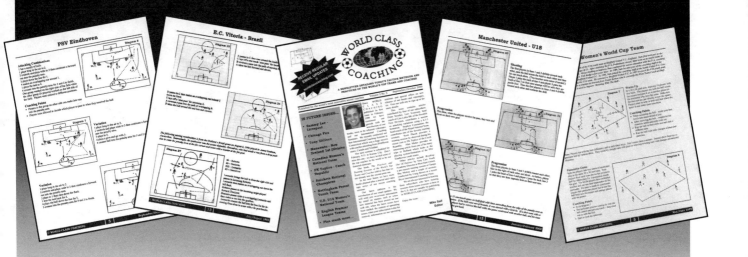